Ancient Epistolary Theorists

SOCIETY OF BIBLICAL LITERATURE
Sources for Biblical Study

Edited by
Bernard Brandon Scott

Number 19
ANCIENT EPISTOLARY THEORISTS

by
Abraham J. Malherbe

Ancient Epistolary Theorists

Abraham J. Malherbe

Scholars Press
Atlanta, Georgia

ANCIENT EPISTOLARY THEORISTS

Abraham J. Malherbe

© 1988
The Society of Biblical Literature

Library of Congress Cataloging in Publication Data

Ancient epistolary theorists.

   (Sources for biblical study ; no. 19)
   Text in Greek and Latin with translations and
notes in English.
   Includes bibliographies and indexes.
   1. Letter-writing, Classical. 2. Classical
letters—History and criticism. 3. Classical
letters—Translations into English. 4. Classical
letters. 5. English letters—Translations from
classical languages. 6. Fathers of the church—
Correspondence. 7. Bible. N.T. Epistles—Language,
style. 8. Rhetoric, Ancient. I. Malherbe, Abraham J.
II. Series.
PA3042.A53   1987   808.6   87-9565
ISBN 1-55540-244-5
ISBN 1-55540-136-8 (alk. paper)

Printed in the United States of America
on acid-free paper

Contents

Preface

This book was originally prepared for a series of publications planned by the Society of Biblical Literature Seminar on the Form and Function of the Pauline Letters (1970–75). When that series did not materialize, the essay was published under the present title in the *Ohio Journal of Religious Studies* (5[1977], 3–77). I have been encouraged to make the material more easily accessible, and am grateful to Professor Derwood C. Smith, editor of that journal, for permission to reprint it, and to Professor Bernard Scott for his willingness to publish it in Sources for Biblical Study. I was aided by Susan Garrett and my wife, Phyllis, in preparing the manuscript for the press. With the exception of new bibliographical entries, minor revision to the translations, and the indexes, no other changes have been made. I am also thankful for permission from the publishers of the texts reproduced here to reprint them. Unless otherwise acknowledged the translations are my own. The book is dedicated to Nils Dahl, who with erudition and wisdom chaired the Seminar in exemplary fashion.

Ancient Epistolary Theorists

Introduction

During the last three decades there has been a renewed interest in the ancient theory and practice of letter writing. The major monographs by Heiki Koskenniemi[1] and Klaus Thraede,[2] concentrating on papyrus and "literary" letters respectively, have been of interest to students of pagan and Christian letters alike. Members of the Society of Biblical Literature have shared that interest in epistolography,[3] and patristic scholars continue to show interest in the great letter writers of Christian antiquity, especially the Cappadocians.[4]

In these studies, reference is made, to varying degrees, to ancient epistolary theory, but the comments are frequently scattered, and no convenient, systematic treatment of ancient epistolary theory is available in English. Nor have the major treatises dealing with the subject ever been translated into a modern language, nor any successful attempt been made to place letter writing in its exact context in rhetorical theory or in school instruction. The present essay is an attempt to meet these needs. It offers the texts and translations of the most important materials dealing with letter writing, and attempts, on the basis of the present state of scholarship on the subject, to locate the place of letter writing in rhetorical theory and in the educational curriculum.

That the material here presented is of interest to specialists in Classics and Patristics need not be argued. Students of the New Testament, however, need to become more aware of this aspect of ancient letter writing, especially as an interest in ancient rhetoric is now being brought to their discipline.[5] The importance of Adolf Deissmann's work for the study of ancient letter writing is universally appreciated.[6] While he has been criticized for his concentration on Greek papyrus letters and his sharp distinction between "letter" and "epistle,"[7] he has continued to exert a strong influence.[8] The present essay, however, represents a different aspect of the subject. Whereas Deissmann was primarily concerned with actual letters, the texts presented here reflect an interest in epistolary theory. Deissmann occasionally referred to the most well known of the texts, but he did not at any length relate the theory they represented to the actual practice of letter writing.[9] Beginnings in that direction have been made,[10] but the material here offered is still to be utilized fully.

I

Epistolary Theory and Rhetoric

Epistolary theory in antiquity belonged to the domain of the rhetoricians, but it was not originally part of their theoretical systems. It is absent from the earliest extant rhetorical handbooks, and it only gradually made its way into the genre.[11] The first extensive discussion of the subject appears in the treatise *De Elocutione,* erroneously attributed in the manuscript tradition to **Demetrius of Phalerum.** The exact date of this treatise is still in dispute, suggestions for it ranging from the third century B.C. to the first century A.D.[12] The sources of the treatise, however, do appear to go back perhaps to the second century, and at the latest, to the first century B.C.[13] What Demetrius has to say on letters is an excursus on the "plain style" (*De Eloc.* 223–235). The discussion is introduced with a reference to a statement attributed to Artemon, the editor of Aristotle's letters, to the effect that a letter should be written in the same manner as a dialogue since a letter is, as it were, one of the two sides of a dialogue (223). Since Aristotle's letters are mentioned elsewhere in the excursus (225, 230, 233, 234), Koskenniemi regards the excursus as representing Artemon's major thoughts on epistolary theory which had originally been contained in an essay introducing the collection of Aristotle's letters.[14] Koskenniemi surmises that Artemon was a contemporary of Theophrastus, and that his epistolary theory had Peripatetic roots. Demetrius is taken to have incorporated the major ideas in Artemon's preface as an excursus in his own work because of the growing interest in letters as well as the neglect of letters in rhetoric. This, however, must remain a surmise. It is not at all certain that anything in the excursus beyond the likening of a letter to one half of a dialogue is to be attributed to him.[15] In view of these uncertainties a sober judgment would appear to be that the earliest extensive discussion of epistolary theory dates from the first century B.C.

That century also saw the work of **Cicero,** who occupies pride of place among Roman letter writers, most of whom were orators.[16] By the time of Cicero Greek grammar and rhetoric had already left their imprint on Rome. The Greek private letter had assumed a definite form and presumably had attracted the attention of the rhetoricians.[17] In any case, what is significant is that Greek and Latin epistolography are of a piece, and that the latter bears testimony to the development of epistolary theory.[18] The exact degree of Cicero's indebtedness to Greek epistolary theorists is difficult to determine. He distinguishes between public and private letters (*Pro Flacco* 16, 37), speaks of *genera epistularum* (*Ad Fam.* 4, 13, 1), and of the inappropriateness of jesting (*iocari*) in a certain type of letter (*Ad Att.* 6, 5, 4), and describes a letter as a conversation with a friend (*Ad Att.* 8, 14, 1) and as mediating the presence of an absent friend (*Ad Fam.* 3, 11, 2). On the basis of such statements H. Peter claimed that Cicero knew a well rounded out Greek system which is reflected in his letters.[19] Cicero did know rhetorical prescriptions on letters and was probably familiar with handbooks on letter writing.[20] To that extent he does show many points of contact with Greek letter theory, but his comments on the types of letters are not the basis for an epistolographic system, nor are they part of such a system. They are rather practical, conventional means of finding an appropriate form for important situations to which letters are addressed. They are general in character and contain nothing specifically theoretical. In view of the points of contact that he does have with the theorists, however, Cicero is an important secondary source for the illumination of epistolary theory.[21]

In the first century A.D. **Seneca,** too, reflects an awareness of descriptions of letters which had become traditional without his betraying any knowledge of an entire theoretical system.[22] Towards the end of the century, in his treatise on the education of an orator, Quintilian in passing mentions the style appropriate to a letter (9, 4, 19f), and his younger contemporary, Theon of Alexandria, in his work on the elementary school exercises in rhetoric, names letter writing as an exercise in characterization (II, 115, 22 Spengel).[23]

It is thus clear that letter writing was of interest to rhetoricians, but it appears only gradually to have attached itself to their rhetorical systems. The discussion in Demetrius is an excursus, Cicero makes no room for a systematic discussion of it in his works on rhetoric, and the references in Quintilian and Theon are casual. This omission is striking in light of the fact that sophists quite regularly occupied the position of *ab epistulis* in chanceries.[24] The failure of such a sophist to write in the proper style could become grounds for an attack on him by other, antagonistic sophists, as the biographer Philostratus reveals to us. Aspasius of Ravenna, while serving as *ab epistulis graecis* in the first half of the third century A.D., incurred the displeasure of, among other sophists, **Philostratus of Lemnos,** who aimed a short work on how to write letters at Aspasius.[25] The tractate seems to have enjoyed wide circulation, as the debt to it of **Gregory of Nazianzus** (*ep.* 51) and the handbook on epistolary style, attributed sometimes to **Libanius** and sometimes to Proclus, would indicate. Yet the subject was not part of a system of rhetoric.

The first rhetorician to discuss the subject as part of the *ars rhetorica* was **Julius Victor** (fourth century).[26] At the end of his handbook he adds two appendices, *de sermocinatione* and *de epistulis,* in which he uses material from traditional rhetorical instruction.[27] While epistolary style is here, then, part of a rhetorical system, it can nevertheless be argued that its relegation to an appendix shows that it does not properly belong in a discussion of rhetoric.[28]

The proper style in which letters should be written is, however, extensively discussed in two handbooks devoted entirely to the subject. They still further reveal the interest of rhetoricians in letter writing. However, while the discus-

sions of letter writing in these manuals are systematic, there is no evidence
to indicate that they were part of a rhetorical system. One handbook is en-
titled *Typoi Epistolikoi,* and is falsely attributed to **Demetrius of Phalerum,**
and the other, the *Epistolimaioi Characteres,* is imputed alternatively to **Libanius** or Proclus the Neoplatonist.

The handbook of **"Demetrius"** is the earlier of the two. Brinkmann
claimed that it was written between 200 B.C. and A.D. 50, likely in the
earlier part of this period,[29] but further investigation has shown that we must
be content with broader limits, between 200 B.C. and A.D. 300, for the text
in its present form.[30] It is likely, however, that the handbook had undergone
a number of revisions before it assumed its present form, and it is possible
that it originated in pre-Christian times.[31]

The manual provides descriptions of twenty-one kinds of letters with an
example of each type. The prologue to the work indicates that in the author's
view the types of styles should be selected and applied with the greatest care.
The manual in its present form is not so much a collection of sample letters
as it is a selection of styles appropriate to different circumstances and a guide
to the tone in which letters are to be written.[32] The descriptions of the letters,
with the examples offered to illustrate the stylistic principles involved, betray
a rhetorical interest in defining various types of exhortation.[33] It aims at meet-
ing the practical needs of its readers, who are assumed to be accomplished
stylists, and not to be in need of instruction in basic rhetorical technique.[34]
Thus, while the manual clearly reflects a rhetorical interest, its primary goal
is nevertheless practical instruction in letter writing, but for advanced students.

The exact relationship of this manual to the actual practice of letter writing
is difficult to determine. The manual originated in Egypt, and many similarities between it and Egyptian papyrus letters can be identified.[35] But this
cannot be taken to prove that this particular manual significantly influenced
actual practice. In Egypt teachers supplied their pupils with model letters to
copy,[36] and it it is reasonable to assume that Greek teachers followed their
example. Model letters, preserved on papyrus, written in 164/3 B.C., would
appear to establish the practice quite early among the Greek-speaking popu-
lation of Egypt.[37]

The bilingual **Bologna Papyrus,** dating from the third or fourth century
A.D., provides further evidence of the popularity of handbooks.[38] It betrays
no interest in theory, but offers eleven samples, in Latin and Greek, of various
types of letters, without introductory descriptions of the types as we find in
"Demetrius". The Latin may be the more original and may have formed the
basis for the Greek, but the artificiality and at times incomprehensibility of
both versions make it likely that the author was at home in neither language.

Rather than being a handbook itself, it appears to be the exercises of a student writing different types of letters, probably following a handbook. An added significance of the papyrus is thus that it witnesses to the modest literary culture of persons who used some of the handbooks.

We thus have two types of handbooks represented by "Demetrius" and reflected in PBon 5, the latter showing no interest in epistolary theory and probably representing fairly elementary practice in letter writing, the former showing greater interest in theory and rhetorical subtleties and probably intended for advanced students.

The handbooks on various levels reflect the traditional and typical elements of letter style,[39] and are therefore valuable as preservers of those traditions, but it would be a mistake to limit their role to reflecting practice and deny that they might also have influenced it.[40] It seems more reasonable that the directions contained in the handbooks were derived from actual practice which was in turn influenced by the manuals through their use in the schools. One should not expect an unrealistic agreement in detail between the handbooks and letters. They did not intend to set forth detailed norms or forms, but presented a framework which allowed for individual creativity.[41]

The *Epistolimaioi Characteres* is variously dated between the fourth and sixth centuries A.D.[42] There are two manuscript traditions of the work, one attributing it to **Libanius,** the other to Proclus. They do not depend on each other, but derive from a common archetype which was produced by neither author. The traditions differ considerably, in title, text, and the arrangement of the contents. That ascribed to Libanius is more widely attested and better transmitted, and has been considered by editors of the work to have been the more original.[43] Despite surface similarities, the differences between this work and that of "Demetrius" are so great that it is not certain that there is any interdependence between the two.

The handbook contains a definition of the letter (1–3), enumerates forty-one types of letters (4) and defines them (5–45), provides instruction on styles (46–51), and adds a brief model of each of the forty-one types of letters (52–93). As the structure of the manual already shows, it basically embodies two kinds of material, theoretical discussions and a collection of sample letters.[44] Both kinds of material show an increasingly rhetorical interest, exhibited not only in the amount of space devoted to them, but also in the precision with which the various types are defined.[45] We have, then, in "Libanius's" handbook a combination and elaboration of the materials on letter writing which we have identified as having been in use in an earlier period.

At the risk of oversimplification, the following appears to have been the development that resulted in the manual, and which would continue to exert great influence in the Byzantine period.[46]

The collections of sample letters, utilized by PBon 5 and the collection incorporated in and elaborated by "Demetrius," were designed for use by the less educated in learning how to write letters. The theoretical discussions, however, are found in the writings of such rhetorically cultured writers as the Demetrius of the *De Elocutione* (and Artemon), Cicero, Philostratus, and Gregory of Nazianzus. Such writers were aware of the diversity of types of letters, and were concerned with their style, but, although they must have known the collections of letters or handbooks in their rudimentary form, they did not need their guidance. The two major handbooks on letter writing combine these two types of material and elaborate them, "Demetrius" to a lesser and "Libanius" to a greater degree.[47] That they provide us with the most extensive theoretical treatment of letters does not mean, however, that their purpose was not practical. To determine that purpose more precisely we must attempt to place letter writing in the educational curriculum.

Letter Writing in the Schools

We do not know the extent to which exercises in letter writing were part of the school curriculum, but it is likely that epistolary form was taught on the basis of model letters in the secondary stage of education.[48] During this stage, boys twelve to fifteen years of age were instructed by the *grammaticus* in the seven liberal arts, with the language arts of the trivium predominating.[49] Instruction in schools utilized handbooks extensively,[50] and it is possible that the type of handbook represented by PBon 5 was used at this level, although it might have been used after the most basic form of the letter had been mastered. We also know that grammar was a major subject in secondary school education,[51] and it is significant that the grammatical handbooks of Dionysius of Alexandria (first century A.D.) and Apollonius Dyscolus (second century A.D.) show an interest in epistolary form from the viewpoint of grammar.[52] The grammatical handbooks, however, may not have been used in actual instruction in letter writing.[53] They clearly presuppose a knowledge of basic forms which must therefore have been learned very early in secondary education.

The majority of papyrus letters also point to elementary instruction in letter writing early in secondary education. That the basic characteristics of the private letter are so faithfully preserved from the fifth century B.C. can only be explained as partly due to school instruction and the guides to letter writing. Most of these letters are written in the kind of school language used by persons of average, superficial education, who painfully attempt to write in an educated manner.[54] The interest at this level would have been in grammar and form rather than style. Instruction in style came at the end of the secondary school curriculum, when the *grammaticus* might put his students through the preliminary rhetorical exercises.

In theory, instruction in the preparatory rhetorical exercises was the work of the teacher of rhetoric to whom pupils would go after completing their education under the *grammaticus*. In fact, however, as rhetoric became increasingly technical, some of the elementary exercises or *progymnasmata* were taken over by the *grammaticus*.[55] Although they are referred to as early as the fourth century B.C., the oldest surviving *progymnasmata* were written by Theon, the contemporary of Quintilian.[56] The *progymnasmata* consisted of a series of carefully graded exercises which progressed from the easy to the more difficult, with each exercise building on the preceding one. Of special interest are the exercises in characterization or impersonation, most commonly called *prosopopoeia*.[57]

Prosopopoeia was one of the later elementary exercises in the series, and was not readily relinquished to the *grammaticus* by the teacher of rhetoric. Quintilian, for example, knows of some *grammatici* who presumed to undertake instruction in the exercise, but objects on the grounds of its difficulty.[58] This means that an interest in letter writing from the viewpoint of style can be identified, perhaps toward the end of the secondary school curriculum, but more likely, at the beginning of the tertiary stage, under the teacher of rhetoric. It should be noted that the purpose of the exercise was not to learn how to write letters, but to develop facility in adopting various kinds of style. One might expect that it was at this point that epistolary theory would be introduced, but the evidence is too slender to make a confident judgment.[59] Nor can we assign the handbooks of "Demetrius" and "Libanius" to this point in the curriculum.[60] Their aim is letter writing itself, to instruct their readers in writing different kinds of letters in styles appropriate to the particular epistolary situation envisioned, while in *prosopopoeia* letter writing is subordinate to another goal.

It is more likely that the handbooks were used in the training of professional letter writers. Their occupations required them to be familiar with both official and rhetorical styles, and the comparative similarity that does exist in their letters suggests that they had received instruction in the subject.[61] The criticism by Philostratus of Lemnos of Aspasius, when compared with other theorists, further shows the degree to which the observance of rhetorical niceties was expected of them. It is natural to assume that such instruction of these professional writers as did exist took place under teachers of rhetoric.[62] The handbook of "Demetrius" is addressed to a person composing official letters, and it is possible that that of "Libanius" has a similar audience in mind. That they almost exclusively contain definitions and sample letters which are private rather than official, simply points to the fact that the official style developed out of the private.[63]

Notes

1. H. Koskenniemi, *Studien zur Idee und Phraseologie des griechischen Briefes bis 400 n. Chr.* (Annales Academiae scientiarum fennicae, Series B, Vol. 102,2; Helsinki: Suomalainen Tiedeakatemian, 1956).
2. K. Thraede, *Grundzüge griechisch-römische Brieftopik* (Monographien zur klassischen Altertumswissenschaft 48; Munich: Beck, 1970).
3. Especially noticeable have been the work done by the Seminar on the Form and Function of the Pauline Letters (1970–75) under the chairmanship of Nils A. Dahl, and the work of the Ancient Epistolography Group (1975–79) under the leadership of John L. White.
4. On Basil, see A. Cavallin, *Studien zu den Briefen des Hl. Basilius* (Lund: Gleerup, 1944) and R. C. Gregg, *Consolation Philosophy: Greek and Christian Paideia in Basil and the Two Categories* (Patristic Monograph Series 3; Cambridge, Mass.: Philadelphia Patristic Foundation, 1975). On Gregory of Nazianzus, see M. Guignet, *Les procédés épistolaires de Saint Gregoire de Nazianze* (Paris: A. Picard, 1911); G. Przychocki, *De Gregorii Nazianzeni epistulis quaestiones selectae* (Cracow: Polish Academy, 1912); R. R. Ruether, *Gregory of Nazianzus: Rhetor and Philosopher* (Oxford: Clarendon, 1969), esp. 124–28. See also W. Erdt, *Christentum und heidnisch-antike Bildung bei Paulin von Nola* (Meisenheim: Anton Hain, 1976).
5. Cf. A. J. Malherbe, *Social Aspects of Earlier Christianity* (2nd ed., enlarged; Philadelphia: Fortress Press, 1983), esp. 57–58, 117. Notable is the work of H. D. Betz, *Galatians* (Hermeneia; Philadelphia: Fortress Press, 1979). For an approach by a specialist in ancient rhetoric, see G. A. Kennedy, *New Testament Interpretation through Rhetorical Criticism* (Chapel Hill and London: Univ. of North Carolina Press, 1984).
6. His work is most conveniently available in his *Bible Studies* (Edinburgh: T. & T. Clark, 1901) and *Light from the Ancient East*, fourth comp. rev. ed. (New York: George H. Doran, 1927; repr. Grand Rapids, Mich., 1965). For discussions of ancient letter writing from the perspective of New Testament scholarship, see W. G. Doty, *Letters in Primitive Christianity* (Guides to Biblical Scholarship 7; Philadelphia: Fortress Press, 1973); N. A. Dahl, "Letter," *Interpreter's Dictionary of the Bible, Supplement* (1976), 538–41; J. L. White, "New Testament Epistolary Literature in the Framework of Ancient Epistolography," *Aufstieg und Niedergang der römischen Welt*, ed. W. Haase & H. Temporini (Berlin: De Gruyter, 1984), 2.25/2, 1730–56; K. Berger, "Hellenistische Gattungen im Neuen Testament," *ibid.*, 1326–63, esp. the trenchant comments (1333–40) on the questions raised by the approach of New Testament scholars.
7. See esp. Thraede, *Gründzuge*, 1–4.
8. Cf. J. C. Hurd, *The Origins of I Corinthians* (New York: Seabury, 1965; reprinted, Macon, Georgia: Mercer Univ., 1983) 3–4.
9. E.g., *Bible Studies*, 4–6, 35; *Light from the Ancient East*, 177–8, 191, 228, 296.
10. See H. Windisch, *Der zweite Korintherbrief* (Göttingen: Vandenhoeck & Ruprecht, 1924) 75, 82, 84, 211, 221, 414; K. Thraede, "Untersuchungen zum Ursprung und zur Geschichte der christlichen Poesie II," *Jahrbuch für Antike und Christentum* 5 (1962) 141–145; Betz, *Galatians*, 14–15, 223, 232–33; idem, *2 Corinthians 8 and 9* (Hermeneia; Philadelphia: Fortress Press, 1985), 129–40; M. Bunker, *Brieformular und rhetorische Disposition im I. Korintherbrief* (Göttingen: Vandenhoeck & Ruprecht, 1984). The most important recent work to place Christian practice in its broader context is S. K. Stowers, *Letter Writing in Greco-Roman Antiquity* (Philadelphia: Westminster Press, 1986).
11. On epistolary theory, see G. Przychocki, *De Gregorii Nazianzeni epistulis;* J. Sykutris, "Epistolographie," *R. E. Suppl.* V (1931), 185–220; Koskenniemi, *Studien*, 18–53; W. G. Mueller, "Der Brief als Spiegel der Seele: Zur Geschichte eines Topos der Epistolartheorie von der Antike bis zu Samuel Richardson," *Antike und Abendland* 26(1980), 138–44; M. A. Marcos Casquero, "Epistolografia romana," *Helmantica* 34(1983), 377–406; J. L. White, *Light from Ancient Letters* (Philadelphia: Fortress Press, 1986), 189–91. On the earliest rhetorical handbooks, see G. A. Kennedy, *The Art of Persuasion in Greece* (Princeton: Princeton Univ., 1963), 54–62, 69–74, passim.
12. For the early dating, see G. M. A. Grube, ed. and trans., *A Greek Critic: Demetrius on Style* (Toronto: Univ. of Toronto, 1961), and idem, *The Greek and Roman Critics* (London:

Methuen, 1965) 110–121. W. Rhys Roberts in his Loeb edition ([London: W. Heinemann, 1932] 270–31) identifies the author as Demetrius of Tarsus (first century A.D.).

13. Thus D. M. Schenkeveld, *Studies in Demetrius on Style* (Amsterdam: A. M. Hakkert, 1964) 135–48, who holds that Demetrius wrote in the first century A.D., but did not adapt his sources to theories current in his own day.

14. *Studien*, 24–27.

15. Thraede, *Grundzüge*, 20–21. He also questions the Peripatetic origin of the theory.

16. E. Bickel, *Lehrbuch der Geschichte der römischen Literatur* (Heidelberg: C. Winter, 1937) 380.

17. H. Koskenniemi, "Cicero über die Briefarten (*genera epistularum*)," *Arctos* (1954) 97–102.

18. A major contribution of Thraede's work is that he has brought the Latin letters into the discussion.

19. H. Peter, *Der Brief in der römischen Literatur* (Leipzig: Teubner, 1901) 22.

20. C. W. Keyes, "The Greek Letter of Introduction," *American Journal of Philology* 56 (1935) 44.

21. H. Rabe, "Aus Rhetoren-Handschriften," *Rheinisches Museum* 64 (1909) 291 n. 2; Koskenniemi, "Cicero über die Briefarten," 101–2 and *Studien*, 32–33; Thraede, *Grundzügen*, 27–47.

22. E.g. *Epp.* 40,1; 67,2; 75,1f. See Thraede, *Grundzüge*, 65–74.

23. Cf. G. A. Kennedy, *The Art of Rhetoric in the Roman World, 300 B. C.—A.D. 300* (Princeton: Princeton Univ., 1972) 487–514 on Quintilian, 615–16 on Theon.

24. See Philostratus, *V.S.* 590; 607; Eunapius, *V.S.* 497, and the discussions in G. W. Bowersock, *Greek Sophists in the Roman Empire* (Oxford: Clarendon, and New York: Oxford, 1969), 44, 50–57.

25. See *V.S.* 628, and Bowersock, *Greek Sophists*, 92, on the controversy. C. L. Kayser, *Flavii Philostrati Opera* (Leipzig: Teubner, 1871) II. 257, 29–258, 28, prints the tractate separately from the letters of Philostratus. In earlier editions it had been printed as the first letter.

26. 447, 35–448, 36 Halm. Cf. L. Radermacher in *R.E.* X (1918), 872–79, esp. 872–73.

27. Cf. Koskenniemi, *Studien*, 31–32. One of his sources may have been Julius Titian, the younger contemporary of Fronto, who was known for his imitation of Cicero's letters.

28. Cf. Rabe, "Aus Rhetoren-Handschriften," 290, who points out that the *Excerpta Rhetorica* 589, 3ff. Halm, also adds an appendix *de epistulis*.

29. L. Brinkmann, "Der älteste Briefsteller," *Rheinisches Museum* 64(1909) 310–17. He was followed, with some modification, by V. Weichert, *Demetrii et Libanii qui feruntur Τύποι Ἐπιστολικοί et'Επιστολιμαῖοι Χαρακτῆρες* (Leipzig: Teubner, 1910), 1–12, and B. Olsson, *Papyrusbriefe aus der frühesten Römerzeit* (Uppsala: Almqvist & Wiksells, 1925), 7–9.

30. Keyes, "The Greek Letter of Introduction," 28–32; Koskenniemi, *Studien*, 54–55.

31. Thraede, *Grundzüge*, 26.

32. Koskenniemi, *Studien*, 62.

33. A comparison with Clement of Alexandria, *Paed.* Bks. I, VIII and IX is instructive, e.g. Demetrius #3 (μεμπτικός) with *Paed.* IX 77, 3ff. (*GCS* 135, 11ff.); Demetrius #6 (ἐπιτιμητικός) with *Paed.* IX 77, 1ff. (*GCS* 134, 33ff.); Demetrius #7 (νουθετητικός) with *Paed* IX 76, 1–4 (*GCS* 134, 13ff.). Clement gives a definition of the particular type of exhortation and illustrates it with Scriptural quotations. On the hortatory tradition, see P. Hartlich, *Exhortationum (προτρεπτικῶν) a Graecis Romanisque scriptarum historia et indoles* (*Leipziger Studien* XI [1889]); T. C. Burgess, *Epideictic Literature* (Chicago: Univ. of Chicago, 1902).

34. Brinkmann, "Der älteste Briefsteller," 313; Koskenniemi, *Studien*, 62–63.

35. Brinkmann, "Der älteste Briefsteller," 311–17; Weichert, *Demetrii et Libanii* XIX–XX; Olsson, *Papyrusbriefe*, 7–10. For a classification of non-papyrus letters into some of the types represented in the handbooks, see M. M. Wagner, "A Chapter in Byzantine Epistolography: The Letters of Theodoret of Cyrus," *Dumbarton Oaks Papers* IV (1948), 119–81; E. M. Cawley, *The Literary Theory and Style of Marcus Cornelius Fronto*, Ph.D. Diss., Tufts Univ., 1971; Stowers, *Letter Writing*.

36. Cf. A. Erman, *Die Literatur der Aegypter* (Leipzig: J. C. Hinrichs, 1923) 252, 257, 260.

37. PParis 63 contains four such letters. The texts are published as numbers 110, 144, 145 and

111, and commented upon, by U. Wilcken, *Urkunden der Ptolemäerzeit (Ältere Funde)* I (Berlin/ Leipzig: W. de Gruyter, 1927). For their use as school exercises, see W. Schmid, "Ein epistolographisches Übungsstuck," *Neue Jahrbücher f. Philol. u. Paedag.* 145 (1892) 692–99, and further, Koskenniemi, *Studien,* 57–59.

38. *Papyri Bononienses I,* editi e commentati da O. Montevecchi (Milan: Vitae a Pensiero, 1953), 18ff., with a note by R. Merkelbach on pp. 19–20 n. 1.

39. Keyes, "The Greek Letter of Introduction," 30, explains the many revisions of "Demetrius'" work as due to a tendency constantly to "improve" the handbook by bringing it into closer agreement with the fashion of the reviser's own times.

40. As is done by Koskenniemi, *Studien,* 61–63.

41. Thraede, *Grundzüge,* 9, 12 n. 21.

42. See the literature cited by Koskenniemi, *Studien,* 56.

43. H. Hinck, "Die Ἐπιστολιμαῖοι Χαρακτῆρες des Pseudo-Libanios," *Neue Jahrbücher f. Philol. u. Paedag.* 99(1869) 537–62; Weichert, *Demetrii et Libanii;* R. Foerster, *Libanii opera,* vol. 9 (Leipzig:Teubner, 1927). J. Sykutris, "Proclos Περὶ Ἐπιστολιμαίου," *Byzantinisch-Neugr. Jahrbücher* 7 (1928–29), 108–18, argues that the form ascribed to Proclus is the more original. He is followed by Koskenniemi, *Studien,* 56.

44. See Rabe, "Aus Rhetoren-Handschriften," 296–303, and, with modifications, Sykutris, "Proklos," 116–18.

45. For example, while "Libanius" does not include a description or an example of the letter of advice (συμβουλευτικός) as "Demetrius" does (#11), in his description of the paraenetic letter (#1) he takes issue with those who equate the two. That the distinction was a topic of interest to rhetorical theorists is widely recognized. Cf. Syranus, *Scholia in Hermogenem* II, 192 Rabe, and for the genre, Josephus Klek, *Symbyleutici qui dicitur sermonis historiam criticam per quattuor saecula continuatam* (Paderborn: C. Schoeningh, 1919).

46. See Rabe, "Aus Rhetoren-Handschriften"; H. Hunger, *Die hochsprachliche Literatur der Byzantiner,* HAW 12.5 (Munich: C. H. Beck, 1978), 1.199–213; K. Krautter, "Acsi ore ad os . . . Eine mittelalterliche Theorie des Briefes und ihr antiker Hintergrund," *Antike und Abendland* 28(1982), 155–68.

47. Rabe, Brinkmann, and Sykutris tend to stress the practical interest of "Demetrius" to the neglect of his rhetorical interest. Koskenniemi, *Studien,* 62–63, is correct in his claim that both handbooks presuppose some rhetorical skill and that they are dealing with subtleties.

48. W. Schubart, *Einführung in die Papyruskunde* (Berlin: Weidmann 1918) 397. The traditional view of education presented here holds that there were three stages through which students progressed: the "primary" school, where elementary instruction in reading and writing was given, the "secondary" or "grammar" school, where students were instructed in language and literature, and the school of rhetoric. For this structure, see H. I. Marrou, *A History of Education in Antiquity* (New York: American Library, 1956); M. L. Clarke, *Higher Education in the Ancient World* (London, 1971); S. F. Bonner, *Education in Ancient Rome* (Berkeley and Los Angeles: Univ. of California, 1977). For a different understanding, see A. D. Booth, "The Schooling of Slaves in First-Century Rome," *Transactions of the American Philological Association* 109(1979), 11–19; R. A. Kaster, "Notes on 'Primary' and 'Secondary' Schools in Late Antiquity," *TAPA* 113(1983) 323–46.

49. Donald L. Clark, *Rhetoric in Greco-Roman Education* (New York: Columbia Univ., 1957) 60–66.

50. See Schubart, *Einführung,* ch. 9; M. Fuhrmann, *Das systematische Lehrbuch* (Göttingen: Vandenhoeck & Ruprecht, 1960).

51. Cf. H. I. Marrou, *History of Education* 235–38, 371–73.

52. See esp. G. A. Gerhard, "Untersuchungen zur Geschichte des griechischen Briefes I. Die Anfangsformel," *Philologus* 64 (1905) 27–65.

53. Rabe, "Aus Rhetoren-Handschriften," 290 n. 1, denies that these handbooks were used in the actual instruction in letter writing.

54. Schubart, *Einführung,* 211. The famous letter of the schoolboy Theon to his father (POxyr. 119), reprinted and discussed by Deissmann, *Light from the Ancient East,* 201–204, with its execrable grammar and spelling, also witnesses to the level on which instruction in letter writing must have been given.

55. On the *progymnasmata*, see Marrou, *History of Education*, 238–42; Clark, *Rhetoric in Greco-Roman Education*, 61–66, 177–212; Kennedy, *The Art of Persuasion*, 269–73; R. F. Hock & E. N. O'Neil, *The Chreia in Ancient Rhetoric. Volume I. The Progymnasmata* (SBL Texts and Translations 27; Atlanta: Scholars Press, 1986), esp. 10–22.

56. II, 59–130 Spengel. For translations of those of Hermogenes (second and third centuries A.D.) and Aphthonius (fourth and fifth centuries A.D.), see C. S. Baldwin, *Medieval Rhetoric and Poetic (to 1400)* (New York: Macmillan, 1928; reprinted, Gloucester, Mass.: Peter Smith, 1959) 23–38 (Hermogenes); R. Nadeau, "The Progymnasmata of Aphthonius," *Speech Monographs* 19 (1952) 264–285.

57. II, 115, 22 Spengel. Cf. Nicolaus of Myra (fifth century A.D.) III, 491, 1ff. Spengel.

58. 1, 9, 6; 2, 1, 1ff.; 3, 8, 49; 9, 2, 29f.; 11, 1, 41.

59. Cf. Quintilian 9, 4, 19f. and Pliny, *Ep.* 7, 9, 7–9. Rabe, "Aus Rhetoren-Handschriften," 289–90, suggests that the exercises might have been prefaced by theoretical observations by the teacher.

60. R. Kassel, *Untersuchungen zur griechischen und römischen Konsolationsliteratur* (Munich: C. H. Beck, 1958) 46–47, assumes that these exercises in *prosopopoeia* provide the background for the fictitious letters of consolation attributed to famous men, e.g. Phalaris, Xenophon, and Julian, but that the handbooks sought to meet the practical needs of letter writers.

61. Schubart, *Einführung*, 198–99, 248.

62. PPar 63 provides evidence that sample letters were used in such schools before Greek rhetoric entered Egypt during the Second Sophistic. Cf. Schmid, "Ein epistolographisches Übungsstuck," 695–96; Wilcken, *Urkunden der Ptolemäerzeit*, I, 474 n. 2; Schubart, *Einführung*, 384–85. But see G. A. Kennedy, *Greek Rhetoric under Christian Emperors* (Princeton: Princeton Univ. Press, 1983), 70–73, who thinks that letter writing was on the fringes of formal education, and surmises that instruction in it might have been given by experienced civil servants.

63. C. B. Welles, *Royal Correspondence in the Hellenistic Period* (New Haven: Yale Univ., 1934) xlii–xliii. See further W. Schubart, "Bemerkungen zum Stile hellenistischer Königsbriefe," *Archiv f. Papyruskunde* 6 (1920) 324–47, and *Einführung*, 211–12.

Summary of Epistolary Theory

Definition of a Letter

A letter is one half of a dialogue (Dem. 223) or a surrogate for an actual dialogue (Cic. *Ad Fam.* 12, 30, 1).

In it one speaks to an absent friend as though he were present (Cic. *Ad Fam.* 2, 4, 1; Sen. *Ep.* 75, 1; Ps. Lib. 2, 58; Jul. Vict.).

The letter is, in fact, speech in the written medium (Cic. *Ad Att.* 8, 14, 1; 9, 10, 1; 12, 53; Sen. *Ep.* 75, 1).

A letter reflects the personality of its writer (Cic. *Ad Fam.* 16, 16, 2; Sen. *Ep.* 40, 1; Dem. 227; Philostr.).

The Subject Matter of a Letter

Letters should be real communications and not technical treatises (Dem. 230–31).

Types of Letters

Cicero distinguishes between *litterae publicae* and *privatae* (*Pro Flacco* 37), and adopts different styles in them (*Ad Fam.* 15, 21, 4). In *Ad Fam.* 2, 4, 1f.; 4, 13, 1; 6, 10, 4, he distinguishes between simple letters with factual information and letters communicating the mood of the writer, which are divided into the *genus familiare et iocosum* and the *genus severum et grave*.

Pseudo Demetrius divides letters into twenty-one types according to their style.

Philostratus, in the conclusion of his discussion, incidentally mentions certain types of style used in letters.

Julius Victor distinguishes between *litterae negotiales* and *familiares*, and prescribes different styles for them.

Pseudo Libanius divides letters into forty-one types according to their style.

Epistolary Style

Letters must be concise.

> Brevity is highly desirable (Dem. 228), but a reaction against overly brief letters can be detected (Greg. Naz. 51, 1–5; Jul. Vict.; Ps. Lib 50). The subject matter should determine length, and clarity, above all, should not be sacrificed for conciseness.

Letters must be clear in what they say.

> Clarity is already a presupposition for other prescriptions in Demetrius (226), and is stressed by the later theorists (Philostr.; Greg. Naz. 51, 4; Jul. Vict.; Ps. Lib. 48–49).

Letters must be adapted to the circumstances and mood of their addresses (Cic. *Ad Fam.* 2, 4, 1; 4, 13, 1; *Ad Att.* 9, 4, 1; Dem. 234; Ps. Dem., proem: Philostr.; Greg. Naz. 51, 4).

Letters should be written in the most appropriate style (Cic. *Ad Fam.* 15, 21, 4; Ps. Lib. 1, 46).

> They should be written in the style of the dialogue (Dem. 223; Quint. 9, 4, 19), but should be natural (Greg. Naz. 51, 5, 7).

> Letters should be written as artistically as possible (Ps. Dem., proem.; Jul. Vict.). According to some theorists they should be written in everyday speech (Cic. *Ad Fam.* 9, 21, 1; Sen. *Ep.* 75, 1), while to others they should be written in a style between the vernacular and Atticism (Philostr.; Ps. Lib. 47; cf. Greg. Naz. 51, 4).

> Disconnected words are frowned upon by Demetrius (226), but asyndeton is praised by Philostratus, *V.S.* 607, as a device that enhances the brilliance of epistolary style.

> While there should be freedom in the structure of a letter, periods should generally be avoided (Dem. 229), and if used at all, should be confined to short letters (Philostr.).

> Covert allusions should not be made (Philostr.). Novel ways of expression should be used, but with discretion (Philostr.).

> Compliments (Dem. 232) and direct address (Jul. Vict.) enliven style.

> Care should be exercised in jesting in a letter. While jesting is appropriate, it should only be indulged in when writing to certain persons, and when the mood is right (Cic., *Ad Fam.* 2, 4, 1; Jul. Vict.).

Introductions and conclusions of letters should be written according to current practice, according to Julius Victor, but Pseudo Libanius (51) reacts against the etiquette of his time.

While the epistolary style is plain (Dem. 223), from the standpoint of expression it is actually a compound of the graceful and plain styles (Dem. 235). It should therefore be characterized by ornamentation (Philostr.; Greg. Naz. 51, 5–7; Ps. Lib. 48; Jul. Vict.), the main characteristic of which is charm. Charm is achieved when the technical philosophical and rhetorical devices are either avoided or used with humor (Greg. Naz. 51, 5–7), and when discreet use is made of histories, myths, literary allusions (Greg. Naz. 51, 5f.; Jul. Vict.; Ps. Lib 50), proverbs and *sententiae* without dialectical subtlety (Dem. 232; Greg. Naz. 51, 5; Jul. Vict.; Ps. Lib. 50). When writing in Latin, Greek words may be used (Jul. Vict.).

Texts and Translations

Demetrius

De Elocutione 223–35 *

[223] Ἐπεὶ δὲ καὶ ὁ ἐπιστολικὸς χαρακτὴρ δεῖται ἰσχνότητος, καὶ περὶ αὐτοῦ λέξομεν. Ἀρτέμων μὲν οὖν ὁ τὰς Ἀριστοτέλους ἀναγράψας ἐπιστολάς φησιν, ὅτι δεῖ ἐν τῷ αὐτῷ τρόπῳ διάλογόν τε
5 γράφειν καὶ ἐπιστολάς· εἶναι γὰρ τὴν ἐπιστολὴν οἷον τὸ ἕτερον μέρος τοῦ διαλόγου.

[224] Καὶ λέγει μέν τι ἴσως, οὐ μὴν ἅπαν· δεῖ γὰρ ὑποκατεσκευ-άσθαι πως μᾶλλον τοῦ διαλόγου τὴν ἐπιστολήν· ὁ μὲν γὰρ μιμεῖται αὐτοσχεδιάζοντα, ἡ δὲ γράφεται καὶ δῶρον πέμπεται τρόπον τινά.

10 [225] Τίς γοῦν οὕτως ἂν διαλεχθείη πρὸς φίλον, ὥσπερ ὁ Ἀριστοτέλης πρὸς Ἀντίπατρον ὑπὲρ τοῦ φυγάδος γράφων τοῦ γέροντός φησιν· "εἰ δὲ πρὸς ἁπάσας οἴχεται | γᾶς φυγὰς οὗτος, ὥστε μὴ κατάγειν, δῆλον ὡς τοῖσγε εἰς Ἅιδου κατελθεῖν βουλομένοις οὐδεὶς φθόνος." ὁ γὰρ οὕτως διαλεγόμενος ἐπιδεικνυμένῳ ἔοικεν μᾶλ-
15 λον, οὐ λαλοῦντι.

[226] Καὶ λύσεις συχναὶ ὁποῖαι * * οὐ πρέπουσιν ἐπιστολαῖς· ἀσαφὲς γὰρ ἐν γραφῇ ἡ λύσις, καὶ τὸ μιμητικὸν οὐ γραφῆς οὕτως οἰ-κεῖον, ὡς ἀγῶνος, οἷον ὡς ἐν τῷ Εὐθυδήμῳ· "τίς ἦν, ὦ Σώκρατες, ᾧ χθὲς ἐν Λυκείῳ διελέγου; ἦ πολὺς ὑμᾶς ὄχλος περιειστήκει." καὶ μι-
20 κρὸν προελθὼν ἐπιφέρει, "ἀλλά μοι ξένος τις φαίνεται εἶναι, ᾧ διε-λέγου· τίς ἦν;" ἡ γὰρ τοιαύτη πᾶσα ἑρμηνεία καὶ μίμησις ὑποκριτῇ πρέποι μᾶλλον, οὐ γραφομέναις ἐπιστολαῖς.

*Text: *Demetrius: On Style*. Edited and translated by W. Rhys Roberts (Loeb Classical Library; rev. ed.; Cambridge, Mass.: Harvard University Press, 1932).

16

Demetrius

On Style 223–235   *(First century B. C.—first century A. D.?)*

[223] We will next treat of the epistolary style, since it too should be plain. Artemon, the editor of Aristotle's *Letters,* says that a letter ought to be written in the same manner as a dialogue, a letter being regarded by him as one of the two sides of a dialogue.

[224] There is perhaps some truth in what he says, but not the whole truth. The letter should be a little more studied than the dialogue, since the latter reproduces an extemporary utterance, while the former is committed to writing and is (in a way) sent as a gift.

[225] Who (one may ask) would, in conversation with a friend, so express himself as does Aristotle when writing to Antipater on the subject of the aged exile? "If he is doomed to wander to the uttermost parts of the earth, an exile hopeless of recall, it is clear that we cannot blame men (like him) who wish to return to home—to Hades." (Fr. 615). A man who conversed in that fashion would seem not to be talking but to be making an oratorical display.

[226] Frequent breaks in a sentence such as . . . are not appropriate in letters. Such breaks cause obscurity in writing, and the gift of imitating conversation is less appropriate to writing than to a speech in debate. Consider the opening of the *Euthydemus:* "Who was it, Socrates, with whom you were conversing yesterday in the Lyceum? Quite a large crowd was surrounding your party." And a little further on Plato adds: "Nay, he seems to me to be some stranger, the man with whom you were conversing. Who was he, pray?" (*Euthyd.* 271A). All such imitative style better suits an actor; it does not suit written letters.

[227] Πλεῖστον δὲ ἐχέτω τὸ ἠθικὸν ἡ ἐπιστολή, ὥσπερ καὶ ὁ διάλογος· σχεδὸν γὰρ εἰκόνα ἕκαστος τῆς ἑαυτοῦ ψυχῆς γράφει τὴν ἐπιστολήν. καὶ ἔστι μὲν καὶ ἐξ ἄλλου λόγου παντὸς ἰδεῖν τὸ ἦθος τοῦ γράφοντος, ἐξ οὐδενὸς δὲ οὕτως, ὡς ἐπιστολῆς.

5 [228] Τὸ δὲ μέγεθος συνεστάλθω τῆς ἐπιστολῆς, ὥσπερ καὶ ἡ λέξις. αἱ δὲ ἄγαν μακραί, καὶ προσέτι κατὰ τὴν ἑρμηνείαν ὀγκωδέστεραι, οὐ μὰ τὴν ἀλήθειαν ἐπιστολαὶ γένοιντο ἄν, ἀλλὰ συγγράμματα, τὸ χαίρειν ἔχοντα προσγεγραμμένον, καθάπερ τοῦ Πλάτωνος πολλαὶ καὶ ἡ Θουκυδίδου.

10 [229] Καὶ τῇ συντάξει μέντοι λελύσθω μᾶλλον· γελοῖον γὰρ περιοδεύειν, ὥσπερ οὐκ ἐπιστολήν, ἀλλὰ δίκην γράφοντα· καὶ οὐδὲ γελοῖον μόνον, ἀλλ᾽ οὐδὲ φιλικὸν (τὸ γὰρ δὴ κατὰ τὴν παροιμίαν "τὰ σῦκα σῦκα" λεγόμενον) ἐπιστολαῖς ταῦτα ἐπιτηδεύειν.

[230] Εἰδέναι δὲ χρή, ὅτι οὐχ ἑρμηνεία μόνον, ἀλλὰ καὶ πράγματά
15 τινα ἐπιστολικά ἐστιν. Ἀριστοτέλης γοῦν ὃς μάλιστα ἐπιτετευχέναι δοκεῖ τοῦ [αὐτοῦ] ἐπιστολικοῦ, "τοῦτο δὲ οὐ γράφω σοί," φησίν. "οὐ γὰρ ἦν ἐπιστολικόν."

[231] Εἰ γάρ τις ἐν ἐπιστολῇ σοφίσματα γράφοι καὶ φυσιολογίας, γράφει μέν, οὐ μὴν ἐπιστολὴν γράφει. φιλοφρόνησις γάρ τις βούλεται
20 εἶναι ἡ ἐπιστολὴ σύντομος, καὶ περὶ ἁπλοῦ πράγματος ἔκθεσις καὶ ἐν ὀνόμασιν ἁπλοῖς.

[232] Κάλλος μέντοι αὐτῆς αἵ τε φιλικαὶ φιλοφρονήσεις καὶ πυκναὶ παροιμίαι ἐνοῦσαι· καὶ τοῦτο γὰρ μόνον ἐνέστω αὐτῇ σοφόν, διότι δημοτικόν τί ἐστιν ἡ παροιμία καὶ κοινόν, ὁ δὲ γνωμολογῶν καὶ
25 προτρεπόμενος οὐ δι᾽ ἐπιστολῆς ἔτι λαλοῦντι ἔοικεν, ἀλλὰ μηχανῆς.

[233] Ἀριστοτέλης μέντοι καὶ ἀποδείξεσί που χρῆται ἐπιστολικῶς, οἷον διδάξαι βουλόμενος, ὅτι ὁμοίως χρὴ εὐεργετεῖν τὰς μεγάλας πόλεις καὶ τὰς μικράς, φησίν, "οἱ γὰρ θεοὶ ἐν ἀμφοτέραις ἴσοι, ὥστ᾽ ἐπεὶ αἱ χάριτες θεαί, ἴσαι ἀποκείσονταί σοι παρ᾽ ἀμφοτέραις." καὶ
30 γὰρ τὸ ἀποδεικνύμενον αὐτῷ ἐπιστολικὸν καὶ ἡ ἀπόδειξις αὐτή.

[234] Ἐπεὶ δὲ καὶ πόλεσίν ποτε καὶ βασιλεῦσιν γράφομεν, ἔστωσαν τοιαῦται [αἱ] ἐπιστολαὶ μικρὸν ἐξηρμέναι πως. στοχαστέον γὰρ καὶ τοῦ προσώπου ᾧ γράφεται· ἐξηρμένη μέντοι [καὶ] οὐχ ὥστε σύγγραμμα εἶναι ἀντ᾽ ἐπιστολῆς, ὥσπερ αἱ Ἀριστοτέλους πρὸς Ἀλέξαν-
35 δρον, καὶ πρὸς τοὺς Δίωνος οἰκείους ἡ Πλάτωνος.

[235] Καθόλου δὲ μεμίχθω ἡ ἐπιστολὴ κατὰ τὴν ἑρμηνείαν ἐκ δυοῖν χαρακτήροιν τούτοιν, τοῦ τε χαρίεντος καὶ τοῦ ἰσχνοῦ. καὶ περὶ ἐπιστολῆς μὲν τοσαῦτα, καὶ ἅμα περὶ τοῦ | χαρακτῆρος τοῦ ἰσχνοῦ.

[227] The letter, like the dialogue, should abound in glimpses of character. It may be said that everybody reveals his own soul in his letters. In every other form of composition it is possible to discern the writer's character, but none so clearly as in the epistolary.

[228] The length of a letter, no less than its style, must be kept within due bounds. Those that are too long, and further are rather stilted in expression, are not in sober truth letters but treatises with the heading "My dear So-and-So." This is true of many of Plato's, and of that of Thucydides.

[229] There should be a certain degree of freedom in the structure of a letter. It is absurd to build up periods, as if you were writing not a letter but a speech for the law courts. And such laboured letter writing is not merely absurd; it does not even obey the laws of friends, which demand that we should "call a spade a spade," as the proverb has it.

[230] We must also remember that there are epistolary topics, as well as epistolary style. Aristotle, who is thought to have been exceptionally successful in attaining the epistolary manner, says; "I have not written to you on this subject, since it was not fitted for a letter." (Fr. 620).

[231] If anybody should write of logical subtleties or questions of natural history in a letter, he writes indeed, but not a letter. A letter is designed to be the heart's good wishes in brief; it is the exposition of a simple subject in simple terms.

[232] Ornament, however, it may have in the shape of friendly bits of kindly advice, mixed with a few good proverbs. This last is the only philosophy admissible in it—the proverb being the wisdom of a people, the wisdom of the world. But the man who utters sententious maxims and exhortations seems to be no longer talking familiarly in a letter but to be speaking *ex cathedra*.

[233] Aristotle, however, sometimes uses actual proofs, but in the way appropriate to a letter. For instance, wishing to show that large towns and small have an equal claim to be well treated, he says: "The gods are as great in one as in the other; and since the Graces are gods, they will be held as great a treasure by you in one as in the other." (Fr. 609). The point he wishes to prove is fitted for a letter, and so is the proof itself.

[234] Since occasionally we write to States or royal personages, such letters must be composed in a slightly heightened tone. It is right to have regard to the person to whom the letter is addressed. The heightening should not, however, be carried so far that we have a treatise in place of a letter, as is the case with those of Aristotle to Alexander and with that of Plato to Dion's friends.

[235] In general it may be remarked that, from the point of view of expression, the letter should be a compound of these two styles, the graceful and the plain.—So much with regard to letter writing and the plain style.

Cicero*

Epistulae ad Familiares 2, 4, 1

Epistularum genera multa esse non ignoras, sed unum illud certissimum, cuius causa inventa res ipsa est, ut certiores faceremus absentes, si quid esset, quod eos scire aut nostra aut ipsorum interesset. Huius generis litteras a me
5   profecto non exspectas. Tuarum enim rerum domesticos habes et scriptores et nuntios. In meis autem rebus nihil est sane novi. Reliqua sunt epistularum genera duo, quae me magno opere delectant, unum familiare et iocosum, alterum severum et grave. Utro me minus deceat uti, non intelligo. Iocerne tecum per litteras? civem mehercule non puto esse, qui temporibus his ridere
10   possit. An gravius aliquid scribam? quid est, quod possit graviter a Cicerone scribi ad Curionem, nisi de republica? Atque in hoc genere haec mea causa est, ut neque ea, quae sentio audeam, nec quae non sentio, velim scribere.

*Texts: *Cicero: Letters to His Friends*. Edited and translated by W. Glynn Williams (Loeb Classical Library; Cambridge, Mass.: Harvard Univ. Press). Vols. 1 (rev. ed.; 1943); 2 (1928); 3 (rev. ed.; 1954).
    Cicero: Letters to Atticus. Edited and translated by E. O. Winstedt (Loeb Classical Library; Cambridge, Mass.: Harvard Univ. Press). Vols. 2 (1913); 3 (1918).

Cicero

Letters to His Friends 2, 4, 1 *(53 B. C.)*

That there are many kinds of letters you are well aware: there is one kind, however, about which there can be no mistake, for indeed letter writing was invented just in order that we might inform those at a distance if there were anything which it was important for them or for ourselves that they should know. A letter of this kind you will of course not expect from me; for as regards your own affairs you have your correspondents and messengers at home, while as regards mine there is absolutely no news to tell you. There remain two kinds of letters which have a great charm for me, the one intimate and humorous, the other austere and serious. Which of the two it least beseems me to employ, I do not quite see. Am I to jest with you by letter? On my oath, I don't think there is a citizen in existence who can laugh in these days. Or am I to write something more serious? What is there that can possibly be written by Cicero to Curio, in the serious style, except on public affairs? Ah! but in this regard my case is just this, that I dare not write what I feel, and I am not inclined to write what I don't feel.

Epistulae ad Familiares 4, 13, 1

Quaerenti mihi iamdiu, quid ad te potissimum scriberem, non modo certa res
nulla, sed ne genus quidem litterarum usitatum veniebat in mentem. Unam
enim partem et consuetudinem earum epistolarum, quibus, secundis rebus,
5   uti solebamus, tempus eripuerat; perfeceratque fortuna, ne quid tale scribere
possem, aut omnino cogitare. Relinquebatur triste quoddam et miserum, et
his temporibus consentaneum genus litterarum; id quoque deficiebat me; in
quo debebat esse aut promissio auxili alicuius, aut consolatio doloris tui.
Quod pollicerer, non erat. Ipse enim, pari fortuna abiectus, aliorum opibus
10   casus meos sustentabam, saepiusque mihi veniebat in mentem queri, quod ita
viverem, quam gaudere, quod viverem.

Epistulae ad Atticum 9, 4, 1

Ego etsi tam diu requiesco, quam diu aut ad te scribo aut tuas litteras lego,
tamen et ipse egeo argumento epistularum et tibi idem accidere certo scio.
15   Quae enim soluto animo familiariter scribi solent, ea temporibus his exclu-
duntur, quae autem sunt horum temporum, ea iam contrivimus.

Epistulae ad Atticum 8, 14, 1

Non dubito, quin tibi odiosae sint epistulae cotidianae, cum praesertim neque
nova de re aliqua certiorem te faciam neque novam denique iam reperiam
20   scribendi ullam sententiam. Sed, si dedita opera, cum causa nulla esset, ta-
bellarios ad te cum inanibus epistulis mitterem, facerem inepte; euntibus
vero, domesticis praesertim, ut nihil ad te dem litterarum, facere non possum
et simul, crede mihi, requiesco paulum in his miseriis, cum quasi tecum lo-
quor, cum vero tuas epistulas lego, multo etiam magis.

Letters to His Friends 4, 13, 1   *(46 B.C.)*

I have been asking myself for some time past what I had best write to you; but not only does no definite theme suggest itself, but even the conventional style of letter writing does not appeal to me. For one customary branch of correspondence in vogue among us when all was well, has been torn away from us by the hardship of the times, and fortune has effectively debarred me from writing or even contemplating anything of the kind. There still remained a certain style of correspondence appropriate to these times of ours in its gloom and melancholy; but I cannot fall back even upon that. For even that should surely convey either the promise of some substantial help or some consolation for your grief. I have no promise to make; for humiliated as I am by a misfortune like your own, it is only by extraneous assistance that I bear the weight of my afflictions, and my heart is more inclined to deplore the conditions than to rejoice in the fact, of my being alive.

Letters to Atticus 9, 4, 1   *(49 B. C.)*

Though now I rest only so long as I am writing to you or reading your letters, still I am in want of subject matter, and feel sure that you are in the same position, for the present crisis debars us from the free and easy topics of friendly correspondence, and the topics connected with the present crisis we have already exhausted.

Letters to Atticus 8, 14, 1   *(49 B.C.).*

I have no doubt my daily letter must bore you, especially as I have no fresh news, nor can I find any excuse for a letter. If I should employ special messengers to convey my chatter to you without reason, I should be a fool: but I cannot refrain from entrusting letters to folk who are bound for Rome, especially when they are members of my household. Believe me, too, when I seem to talk with you, I have some little relief from sorrow, and, when I read a letter from you, far greater relief.

Epistulae ad Atticum 9, 10, 1

Nihil habebam, quod scriberem. Neque enim novi quicquam audieram et ad
tuas omnes rescripseram pridie. Sed, cum me aegritudo non solum somno
privaret, verum ne vigilare quidem sine summo dolore pateretur, tecum ut
5   quasi loquerer, in quo uno acquiesco, hoe nescio quid nullo argumento pro-
posito scribere institui.

Epistulae ad Atticum 12, 53

Ego, etsi nihil habeo, quod ad te scribam, scribo tamen, quia tecum loqui
videor. Hic nobiscum sunt Nicias et Valerius. Hodie tuas litteras exspectaba-
10 mus matutinas. Erunt fortasse alterae posmeridianae, nisi te Epiroticae litterae impedient; quas ego non interpello. Misi ad te epistulas ad Marcianum
et ad Montanum. Eas in eundem fasciculum velim addas, nisi forte iam de-
disti.

Epistulae ad Familiares 16, 16, 2

15 Si enim mihi Stati fidelitas est tantae voluptati, quanti esse in isto haec eadem
bona debent, additis litteris, sermonibus, humanitate, quae sunt his ipsis
commodis potiora! Amo te omnibus equidem maximis de causis, verum
etiam propter hanc, vel quod mihi sic, ut debuisti, nuntiasti. Te totum in
litteris vidi. Sabini pueris et promisi omnia, et faciam.

Letters to Atticus 9, 10, 1 *(49 B. C.)*

I have nothing to write. There is no news that I have heard, and all your letters I answered yesterday. But as a sick heart not only robs me of sleep, but will not allow me even to keep awake without the greatest pain, I have begun to write to you something or other without any definite subject, that I may have a sort of talk with you, the only thing that gives me relief.

Letters to Atticus 12, 53 *(45 B.C.).*

Though I have nothing to say to you, I write all the same, because I feel as though I were talking to you. Nicias and Valerius are here with me. I am expecting a letter from you early today. Perhaps there will be another in the afternoon, unless your letter to Epirus hinders you: I don't want to interrupt that. I have sent you letters for Marcianus and for Montanus. Please put them in the same packet, unless you have sent it off already.

Letters to His Friends 16, 16, 2 *(54 or 53 B.C.).*

For if Statius's faithful service is so constant a pleasure to me, how inestimable should such good qualities be in your man, when we think too of his literary and conversational powers, and his refinement—merits which outweigh even those qualities which minister to our personal comfort. I have every reason, and each the strongest possible, to love you, and I have this reason also, I mean that you sent me the news in precisely the proper way. All of you was revealed to me in your letter. I have promised Sabinus's serving-men to do all they asked, and I shall do so.

Epistulae ad Familiares 12, 30, 1

Itane? praeter litigatores nemo ad te meas litteras? Multae istae quidem; tu
enim perfecisti, ut nemo sine litteris meis tibi se commendatum putaret; sed
quis umquam tuorum mihi dixit esse, cui darem, quin dederim? aut quid mihi
iucundius, quam, cum coram tecum loqui non possim, aut scribere ad te aut
tuas legere litteras? Illud magis mihi solet esse molestum, tantis me impediri
occupationibus, ut ad te scribendi meo arbitratu facultas nulla detur. Non
enim te epistulis, sed voluminibus lacesserem, quibus quidem me a te pro-
vocari oportebat. Quamvis enim occupatus sis, oti tamen plus habes; aut, si
ne tu quidem vacas, noli impudens esse, nec mihi molestiam exhibere, et a
me litteras crebriores, quum tu mihi raro mittas, flagitare.

Letters to His Friends 12, 30, 1   *(43 B.C.)*.

So that's it? Except litigants, nobody ever brings you a letter from me? Well, it is true that there are heaps of such letters, since you have managed to make everybody believe that unless he has a letter from me, he has brought no recommendation to you; but what friend of yours has ever told me there was anybody to entrust a letter to, but that I did so? Or what could give me greater pleasure, failing a *tête-à-tête* talk with you, than either to write to you, or to read a letter of yours? What often annoys me still more is my being tied up with such pressing engagements that I find it impossible to write to you when the spirit moves me. For it is not with epistles so much as with volumes that I should provoke you to retaliation, though it is by such means that you ought to have challenged me first, seeing that, however busy you have been, you have more leisure than I, or if you have no time either, do show some sense of decency, and don't keep worrying me and brusquely insisting upon my writing often, when you yourself so seldom write to me.

Seneca*

Epistulae Morales 40, 1

Quod frequenter mihi scribis, gratias ago. Nam quo uno modo potes, te mihi
ostendis. Numquam epistulam tuam accipio, ut non protinus una simus. Si
imagines nobis amicorum absentium iucundae sunt, quae memoriam renovant
5   et desiderium falso atque inani solacio levant, quanto iucundiores sunt litterae, quae vera amici absentis vestigia, veras notas adferunt? Nam quod
in conspectu dulcissimum est, id amici manus epistulae inpressa praestat,
agnoscere.

Epistulae Morales 75, 1–2

10 Minus tibi accuratas a me epistulas mitti quereris. Quis enim accurate loqui-
tur, nisi qui vult putide loqui? Qualis sermo meus esset, si una sederemus aut
ambularemus, inlaboratus et facilis, tales esse epistulas meas volo, quae nihil
habent accersitum nec fictum. Si fieri posset, quid sentiam, ostendere quam
loqui mallem. Etiam si disputarem, nec supploderem pedem nec manum iac-
15 tarem nec attollerem vocem, sed ista oratoribus reliquissem, contentus sensus
meos ad te pertulisse, quos nec exornassem nec abiecissem.

*Text: *Seneca: Ad Lucilius Epistulae Morales*. Edited and translated by Richard M. Gummere
(Loeb Classical Library; Cambridge, Mass.: Harvard Univ. Press). Vols. 1 (1928); 2 (1932).
Reprinted by permission of the publishers and The Loeb Classical Library.

Seneca

Moral Epistles 40, I   *(A. D. 63–65)*

I thank you for writing to me so often; for you are revealing your real self to me in the only way you can. I never receive a letter from you without being in your company forthwith. If the pictures of our absent friends are pleasing to us, though they only refresh the memory and lighten our longing by a solace that is unreal and unsubstantial, how much more pleasant is a letter, which brings us real traces, real evidences, of an absent friend! For that which is sweetest when we meet face to face is afforded by the impress of a friend's hand upon his letter—recognition.

Moral Epistles 75, 1–2

You have been complaining that my letters to you are rather carelessly written. Now who talks carefully unless he also desires to talk affectedly? I prefer that my letters should be just what my conversation would be if you and I were sitting in one another's company or taking walks together,—spontaneous and easy; for my letters have nothing strained or artificial about them. If it were possible, I should prefer to show, rather than speak, my feelings. Even if I were arguing a point, I should not stamp my foot, or toss my arms about, or raise my voice; but I should leave that sort of thing to the orator, and should be content to have conveyed my feelings toward you without having either embellished them or lowered their dignity.

Pseudo Demetrius*

Τύποι Ἐπιστολικοί.

Τῶν ἐπιστολικῶν τύπων, ὦ Ἡρακλείδη, ἐχόντων τὴν θεωρίαν τοῦ συνεστάναι μὲν ἀπὸ πλειόνων εἰδῶν, ἀναβάλλεσθαι δὲ ἐκ τῶν ἀεὶ πρὸς τὸ παρὸν ἁρμοζόντων, καὶ καθηκόντων μὲν ὡς τεχνικώτατα
5 γράφεσθαι, γραφομένων δ' ὡς ἔτυχεν ὑπὸ τῶν τὰς τοιαύτας τοῖς ἐπὶ πραγμάτων ταττομένοις ὑπουργίας ἀναδεχομένων, θεωρῶν σε φιλοτίμως ἔχοντα πρὸς φιλομάθειαν ἐπραγματευσάμην διά τινων συστήσειν ἰδεῶν καὶ πόσας καὶ ἃς ἔχουσι διαφοράς, καὶ καθάπερ δεῖγμα τῆς ἑκάστου γένους τάξεως ὑποδέδειχα προσεκθέμενος
10 μερικῶς τὸν περὶ ἑκάστου λόγον, ἅμα μὲν ὑπολαμβάνων καὶ σοὶ τοῦτο κεχαρισμένον ὑπάρχειν, εἴ τι τῶν ἄλλων περισσότερον εἰδήσεις τὸ λαμπρὸν τοῦ βίου τιθέμενος οὐκ ἐν τοῖς βρώμασιν, ἀλλ' ἐν ταῖς ἐπιστήμαις, ἅμα δὲ κἀμὲ νομίζων τοῦ προσήκοντος ἐπαίνου μεθέξειν. οὐ μὴν γένος τι τοιοῦτον καὶ παρὰ τὴν ἡλικίαν ἐφευρίσκων μέθοδον
15 προὐθυμήθην καὶ ταῦτα τῆς περιστάσεως τὸν εὐφυέστατον δυναμένης ἐμποδίζειν. οὐ γὰρ οὕτως ἀποδοχῆς τεύξεται πρεσβύτερος ἀνὴρ πλεῖστον καταναλώσας χρόνον πρὸς μάθησιν, ὡς ὁ τὴν ἐπισφαλῆ καὶ παρακίνδυνον ἡλικίαν πρὸς τὰ κάλλιστα τῶν μαθημάτων καταχρησάμενος; ἴσως μὲν γὰρ αὐτοῖς ὁ χρόνος διαρκῶν εὐχερὴς
20 καθηγητὴς γίνεται τούτων ἐχόντων ποικίλην πειθώ, ὁ δ' αὖ τῆς νεότητος συνίσταται καιρὸς πολλὰς ἔχων δυσχερείας.
Γένη μὲν οὖν ἐστιν, οἷς ἐντετυχήκαμεν, ἓν καὶ εἴκοσι. τάχα δ' ἂν ἐνέγκοι πολλαπλάσια τούτων ὁ χρόνος. εὐφυὴς γὰρ εὑρετὴς καὶ τεχνῶν καὶ θεωρημάτων οὗτος. ἄλλος δὲ τῶν καθ' ἡμᾶς οὐδεὶς
25 ἐπίκαιρος εἰς ἐπιστολικὸν τρόπον ἀνήκων τύπος. ἐπονομάζεται δ' ἕκαστος αὐτῶν ἀφ' ἧς ἐστιν ἰδέας οὕτως· φιλικός, συστατικός, μεμπτικός, ὀνειδιστικός, παραμυθητικός, ἐπιτιμητικός, νουθετη-τικός, ἀπειλητικός, ψεκτικός, ἐπαινετικός, συμβουλευτικός, ἀξιωμα-τικός, ἐρωτηματικός, ἀποφαντικός, ἀλληγορικός, αἰτιολογικός, κατ-
30 ηγορικός, ἀπολογητικός, συγχαρητικός, εἰρωνικός, ἀπευχαριστικός.

*Text: *Demetrii et Libanii qui feruntur ΤΥΠΟΙ ΕΠΙΣΤΟΛΙΚΟΙ et ΕΠΙΣΤΟΛΙΜΑΙΟΙ ΧΑΡΑΚΤΗΡΕΣ*. Edited by Valentin Weichert (Leipzig: Teubner, 1910).

Pseudo Demetrius

Epistolary Types   *(second century B.C.—third century A. D.)*

According to the theory that governs epistolary types, Heraclides, (letters) can be composed in a great number of styles, but are written in those which always fit the particular circumstance (to which they are addresed). While (letters) ought to be written as skillfully as possible, they are in fact composed indifferently by those who undertake such services for men in public office. Since I see that you are eager in your love to learn, I have taken it upon myself, by means of certain styles, to organize and set forth (for you) both the number of distinctions between them and what they are, and have sketched a sample, as it were, of the arrangement of each kind, and have, in addition, individually set forth the rationale for each of them. (I do so), partly assuming that this pleases you too, since you will know that you are making your splendid life surpass others, not in banquets, but in professional skills, and partly believing that I shall share in the praise that will properly (redound to you). In devising such a mode for treating the subject, I did not at all desire to hinder any class (of people) as being too old, and that on the grounds that the circumstances (of old age) can hinder (even) the most highly gifted person. For will not an older person, by following this course of action and lavishing most of his time on learning, meet with approval as one who has fully used his precarious and hazardous age in pursuing the noblest of the sciences? For perhaps as time sustains them it becomes a tolerant teacher of those things that offer diverse means of persuasion, whereas youth's season, on the other hand, is contracted and offers many annoyances.

There are, then, twenty-one kinds that we have come across. Perhaps time might produce more than these, since it is a highly gifted inventor of skills and theories. But as far as we are concerned, there is no other type that properly pertains to the epistolary mode. Each of them is named after the form of style to which it belongs, as follows: friendly, commendatory, blaming, reproachful, consoling, censorious, admonishing, threatening, vituperative, praising, advisory, supplicatory, inquiring, responding, allegorical, accounting, accusing, apologetic, congratulatory, ironic, thankful.

31

[1] Ὁ μὲν οὖν φιλικός ἐστιν ὁ δοκῶν ὑπὸ φίλου γράφεσθαι πρὸς φίλον. γράφουσι δὲ οὐχ οἱ πάντως φίλοι. πολλάκις γὰρ ἐν ὑπάρχοις κείμενοι πρὸς ὑποδεεστέρους ὑπό τινων ἀξιοῦνται φιλικὰ γράψαι καὶ πρὸς ἄλλους ἴσους, στρατηγούς, ἐπιστρατήγους, διοικητάς. ἔστιν ὅτε
5　καὶ προσγράφουσι τούτους ἀγνοοῦντες. οὐ γὰρ διὰ τὸ συγκεκρᾶσθαι καὶ μίαν ἔχειν αἵρεσιν τοῦτο πράττουσιν, ἀλλ᾽ οὐδένα νομίζοντες ἀντ-ερεῖν αὐτοῖς φιλικὰ γράφουσιν, ⟨ἀλλ᾽⟩ ὑπομενεῖν καὶ ποιήσειν περὶ ὧν γράφουσιν. ὁ μέντοι τύπος καλεῖται τῆς ἐπιστολῆς φιλικὸς ὡς πρὸς φίλον γραφόμενος. ἔστι δὲ τοιοῦτος·
10　Εἰ καὶ πολύ σου διάστημα τυγχάνω κεχωρισμένος, τῷ σώματι μόνον πάσχω τοῦτο. οὐδὲ γὰρ οὐδέποτε δυνατὸν ἐπιλαθέσθαι με σοῦ οὐδὲ τῆς γεγονυίας ἡμῖν ἐκ παίδων ἀνεγκλήτου συνανατροφῆς. εἰδὼς δὲ ἐμαυτὸν τὰ πρὸς σὲ γνησίως διακείμενον καὶ πάνυ τὸ σοὶ συμφέρον ἀπροφασίστως ὑπηρετήσαντα τὴν αὐτὴν ὑπείληφα καὶ σὲ περὶ ἐμοῦ
15　γνώμην ἔχοντα κατὰ μηδὲν ἀντερεῖν πρός με. καλῶς οὖν ποιήσεις πυκνότερον ἐπισκοπῶν τοὺς ἐν οἴκῳ μή τινος ἔχωσι χρείαν καὶ συμπαριστάμενος ἐν οἷς ἂν δέωνται καὶ γράφων ἡμῖν περὶ ὧν αἱρῇ.
[2] Ὁ δὲ συστατικός, ὃν ὑπὲρ ἄλλου πρὸς ἄλλον γράφομεν ἔπαινον συγκαταπλέκοντες ἅμα καὶ τοὺς πρότερον ἠγνοημένους λέγοντες ὡς
20　ἐγνωσμένους. οὕτως·
Τὸν δεῖνα τὸν παρακομίζοντά σοι τὴν ἐπιστολὴν καὶ ἡμῖν κεκριμέ-νον καὶ δι᾽ ἣν ἔχει πίστιν ἀγαπώμενον καλῶς ποιήσεις ἀποδοχῆς ἀξιώσας καὶ δι᾽ ἐμὲ καὶ δι᾽ αὐτόν, ἔτι δὲ καὶ διὰ σαυτόν. οὐ μετα-μελήσῃ γὰρ ἐν οἷς θέλεις εἴτε λόγον ἀπόρρητον εἴτε πρᾶξιν εἰπεῖν.
25　ἀλλὰ καὶ σὺ πρὸς ἑτέρους ἐπαινέσεις αὐτὸν αἰσθόμενος ἣν ἐν παντὶ δυνατός ἐστι χρείαν παρασχέσθαι.
[3] Μεμπτικὸς δέ ἐστιν ὁ μὴ νομίζεσθαι βαρεῖν προσδεχόμενος. οἷον·
Εἰ μὴ παραδέδωκέ σοι μηδέπω ὁ καιρὸς ὧν εὖ πέπονθας ἐκτῖσαι
30　χάριτας, οὐδὲ αὐτὸ τοῦτό γε καλῶς ἔχειν ὑπείληφα τὸ μὴ μνημονεύειν ὧν ἔπαθες. σὺ δὲ καὶ δυσχερεῖς καθ᾽ ἡμῶν λόγους προστίθεις. σὲ μὲν οὖν μεμφόμεθα τρόπον ἔχοντα τοιοῦτον, αὐτοὺς δέ, ὅτι σὲ τοιοῦτον ὄντα ἠγνοοῦμεν.

[1] The friendly type, then, is one that seems to be written by a friend to a friend. But it is by no means (only) friends who write (in this manner). For frequently those in prominent positions are expected by some to write in a friendly manner to their inferiors and to others who are their equals, for example, to military commanders, viceroys, and governors. There are times, indeed, when they write to them without knowing them (personally). They do so, not because they are close friends and have (only) one choice (of how to write), but because they think that nobody will refuse them when they write in a friendly manner, but will rather submit and heed what they are writing. Nevertheless, this type of letter is called friendly as though it were written to a friend. It is as follows:

Even though I have been separated from you for a long time, I suffer this in body only. For I can never forget you or the impeccable way we were raised together from childhood up. Knowing that I myself am genuinely concerned about your affairs, and that I have worked unstintingly for what is most advantageous to you, I have assumed that you, too, have the same opinion of me, and will refuse me in nothing. You will do well, therefore, to give close attention to the members of my household lest they need anything, to assist them in whatever they might need, and to write us about whatever you should choose.

[2] The commendatory type, which we write on behalf of one person to another, mixing in praise, at the same time also speaking of those who had previously been unacquainted as though they were (now) acquainted. In the following manner:

So-and-so, who is conveying this letter to you, has been tested by us and is loved on account of his trustworthiness. You will do well if you deem him worthy of hospitality both for my sake and his, and indeed for your own. For you will not be sorry if you entrust to him, in any matter you wish, either words or deeds of a confidential nature. Indeed, you, too, will praise him to others when you see how useful he can be in everything.

[3] The blaming type is one that undertakes not to seem harsh. For example:

Since you have not yet had time to express your thanks for the favors you have received, for that reason I thought it well not to mention what you have received. And yet you are annoyed with us, and impute words (to us). We do, then, blame you for having such a character, and we blame ourselves for not knowing that you were such a man.

[4] Ὀνειδιστικὸς δέ ἐστιν, ὅταν αὖ τὸν ὑφ᾽ αὑτῶν προευεργετημέ-
νον ἐφ᾽ οἷς ἔπραξε μετ᾽ ἐγκλημάτων ὀνειδίζωμεν.
Ἔδει σὲ τὸ γνῶθι σαυτὸν μαθόντα τότε ἑτέροις προσφέρεσθαι
δυσκόλως. νῦν δ᾽ ἀκμὴν ὑφ᾽ ἡμῶν τρεφόμενος καὶ δι᾽ ἡμᾶς ἔχων τὸ
πνεῦμα μεῖζον φρονεῖς τοῦ δέοντος. ἡμεῖς δὲ τούτου αἴτιοι. σὲ γὰρ
ἔδει μὴ τυχεῖν ἐλευθέρου σχήματος. καίπερ οὐδὲ νῦν ἐλεύθερος
γέγονας σχῆμα κεκτημένος δουλοπρεπές.
[5] Παραμυθητικὸς δέ ἐστιν ὁ γραφόμενος τοῖς ἐπὶ λύπης καθεστη-
κόσι δυσχεροῦς τινος γεγονότος. ἔστι δὲ τοιοῦτος·
Ἀκούσας τὰ δεινὰ τῆς ἀχαρίστου σου τύχης ἀπηντημένα καθ᾽
ὑπερβολὴν ἤλγησα νομίσας οὐ σοὶ μᾶλλον ἢ ἐμοὶ συμβεβηκέναι τὸ
γεγονός. ἐκείνην μὲν οὖν τὴν ἡμέραν ἅπαντα ἰδὼν τὰ πρὸς τὸν βίον
ἑστῶτα συνεφόραζον, ἐννοηθεὶς δὲ ὅτι τὰ τοιαῦτα πᾶσίν ἐστιν ὑπο-
κείμενα τῆς φύσεως οὔτε χρόνον οὔτε ἡλικίαν ὑφισταμένης, καθ᾽ ἣν
δεῖ τι πάσχειν, ἀλλ᾽ ἀδήλως μετὰ σκαιότητος οὐκ ἀξίως πολλάκις
ἀπαντώσης, ἐπεὶ μὴ παρὼν τετύχηκα παρακαλεῖν σε, δι᾽ ἐπιστολῆς
ἔκρινα τοῦτο ποιῆσαι. φέρε γοῦν τὸ γεγονὸς ὡς δύνῃ κουφότατα καὶ
καθὼς ἄλλῳ παρήνεσας, σαυτῷ παραίνεσον. ἐπίστασαι γὰρ ὅτι τὸ
μέλλον χρόνῳ κουφιεῖν σε τοῦτο ὁ λόγος εὐμαρέστερον ποιήσει.
[6] Ἐπιτιμητικὸς δέ ἐστιν ὁ ἐφ᾽ ἁμαρτήμασι προγεγονόσι μετ᾽
ἐπιπλήξεως γραφόμενος. οὕτως·
Τῶν ἁμαρτημάτων τὰ μὲν ἑκουσίως γίνεται, τὰ δὲ ἀκουσίως, καὶ τὰ
μὲν μεγάλα καθέστηκε, τὰ δὲ μικρά, καὶ τὰ μὲν μόνοις βλαβερὰ τοῖς
ἁμαρτάνουσι, τὰ δὲ ἑτέροις. σοὶ δὲ καθάπερ ἐπιτήδευμα συμβέβηκεν
ὄντα· καὶ γὰρ οὐκ ἄκων μεγάλα καὶ πολλοῖς βλαβερὰ διαπέπραξαι.
προσήκει μὲν οὖν σε μείζονος ἐπιτυχεῖν ἐπιπλήξεως, εἰ δὴ κατὰ τὸ
παρὸν συντετύχηκε καὶ ἐπὶ ἑτέρων τῶν ἀδικηθέντων. ἀλλ᾽ ἔτι γε δυ-
νατόν ἐστιν ἰάσεως τυχεῖν ⟨τὸ⟩ γεγονὸς πλημμέλημα. πρὸς διόρθωσιν
γὰρ ἀγαγὼν αὐτὸς αἴτιος γενήσῃ τοῦ μὴ γεγονέναι καθάπερ ἔμ-
προσθεν τοῦ γεγονέναι.
[7] Νουθετητικὸς δέ ἐστιν, ὃς καὶ διὰ τῆς ὀνομασίας ὁποῖός ἐστι
δηλοῖ· τὸ γὰρ νουθετεῖν ἐστι νοῦν ἐντιθέναι τῷ νουθετουμένῳ καὶ δι-
δάσκειν τί πρακτέον καὶ μή. οὕτως·
Κακῶς ἐποίησας οὕτω χρησάμενος ἀνδρὶ καλῶς ἀνεστραμμένῳ καὶ
κατὰ λόγον βεβιωκότι καὶ τὸ ὅλον μηδὲν ἄτοπον εἰς σὲ πεποιηκότι.
παραιτήσεως οὖν ἀξίωσον τὸ πρᾶγμα. καὶ γὰρ σὺ πάλιν ὑπ᾽ ἄλλου
παθὼν ῥᾳδίως ἂν ἤνεγκας τόδε ἐπὶ σαυτὸν δικαιῶν. μὴ δόκει οὖν
μήτε γονέων μήτε ἀγωγῆς τετυχηκέναι μήτε τὸ πᾶν ἔσχατον συγγενῆ
τινα ἢ φίλον ἔχειν τὸν ἐπιτιμήσοντα τοῖς ἁμαρτήμασιν.

[4] It is the reproachful type when we once more reproach, with accusations, someone whom we had earlier benefited, for what he has done.

You were bound, when you had just learned (the maxim) "Know yourself," to behave peevishly toward others. But (even) now, although you are (still) being supported by us in the prime of your life, and owe your life to us, you think more highly (of yourself) than you ought. We are to be blamed for this. For you were bound not to attain the character of a freeman. Even now you are not free, for you have acquired a servile character.

[5] The consoling type is that written to people who are grieving because something unpleasant has happened (to them). It is as follows:

When I heard of the terrible things that you met at the hands of thankless fate, I felt the deepest grief, considering that what had happened had not happened to you more than to me. When I saw all the things that assail life, all that day long I cried over them. But then I considered that such things are the common lot of all, with nature establishing neither a particular time or age in which one must suffer anything, but often confronting us secretly, awkwardly and undeservedly. Since I happened not to be present to comfort you, I decided to do so by letter. Bear, then, what has happened as lightly as you can, and exhort yourself just as you would exhort someone else. For you know that reason will make it easier for you to be relieved of your grief with the passage of time.

[6] The censorious type is that written with rebukes on account of errors that have already been comitted. In the following manner:

Some sins are committed voluntarily and some involuntarily, some are major and some minor, some are harmful only to those who commit them, while others are harmful to other people as well. But your sins were like a way of life with you; indeed, you did not unwillingly commit sins that are great and harmful to many. It is therefore fitting that you meet with a more severe rebuke, if indeed in the present case it has happened that others also have been wronged. Nevertheless, the trespass that has occurred can still be set right. For if you aim at correcting your behavior, you yourself will be responsible for its not happening (again) as it did before.

[7] The admonishing type is one which indicates by its name what its character is. For admonition is the instilling of sense in the person who is being admonished, and teaching him what should and should not be done. In the following manner:

You acted badly when you ill-treated a man who had conducted himself well and had lived according to reason and had, generally speaking, done you no harm. Realize, therefore, that this action (of yours) deserves an apology. Indeed, if you had been so treated by someone else, you would have taken it amiss and demanded justice for what had been done to you. Do not, then, think that the person who would rebuke sins had neither parents nor a (proper) upbringing, nor, worst of all, that he has no relative or friend.

[8] Ἀπειλητικὸς δέ ἐστιν, ὅταν μετ' ἐπιτάσεως φόβον τισὶν ἐμποιῶ-
μεν ἐπὶ πεπραγμένοις ἢ πραχθησομένοις. οὕτως·
Εἰ μὲν ὑπολαμβάνεις μηδεμίαν ὑφέξειν δίκην ἐφ' οἷς διαπέπραξαι,
πρᾶττε. εἴσῃ δὲ ἀκριβῶς ὡς οὔτε ἀναπτησόμενος οὔτε καταδυσόμενος
5   οὐδενὶ τρόπῳ χρόνον ἐπισπᾷ κενόν. ὁδὸν γὰρ οὐκ ἂν εὕροις δι' ἧς
ἀποφύγοις ἅ σε δεῖ παθεῖν.
[9] Ψεκτικὸς δέ ἐστιν, ὅταν τρόπου κακίαν ἢ δυσχέρειαν πράξεως
κατά τινος ἐξαγγέλλωμεν. οὕτως·
Ὁ δεῖνα ὡς κέχρηται τοῖς ἐγκεχειρισμένοις ἀνελευθέρως καὶ τῆς
10 προαιρέσεως ἀναξίως, κἂν ἐγὼ σιωπῶ, παρ' ἄλλων ἀκούσῃ· γράφειν
γὰρ προσήκει περὶ ὧν ἂν μή τινες ἐπιστῶνται· περὶ δὲ τῶν ἅπασι φα-
νερῶν καὶ ὑπ' αὐτῆς τῆς φήμης ἀναγγελλομένων περισσόν τι καὶ τὸ
μηνύειν ἃ δι' αὐτῶν ἐλέγχεται σιωπωμένων.
[10] Ἐπαινετικὸς δέ ἐστιν, ὅταν ἐφ' οἷς [ἂν] ἔπραξέ τις ἢ προείλετο,
15 παρακαλῶμεν ἀποδεχόμενοι τὸν τρόπον τοῦτον·
Ἐγὼ καὶ πρότερον εἰ ἔγραψας γράμμασι μετειλήφειν τῆς σῆς
φιλοκαλίας καὶ νῦν ἐφ' οἷς πέπραχας ἀποδέχομαί τε καὶ παρακαλῶ.
συνοίσει γὰρ ἡμῖν ἀμφοτέροις.
[11] Συμβουλευτικὸς δέ ἐστιν, ὅταν τὴν ἰδίαν γνώμην προφερόμενοι
20 προτρέπωμεν ἐπί τι ἢ ἀποτρέπωμεν ἀπό τινος. οἷον οὕτως·
Ἐξ ὧν εὐδοκίμησα διὰ τῶν ἀρχομένων κεφαλαιωδῶς ὑποδέδειχά
σοι. γινώσκω μὲν οὖν ὅτι καὶ σὺ τῷ τρόπῳ δυνατὸς εἶ τὴν παρὰ τῶν
ὑποτεταγμένων εὔνοιαν περιποιεῖσθαι τῶν ὑπηκόων, ἔτι δὲ φίλους
πλείστους μὲν οὐ ποιεῖν, πρὸς ἅπαντας δὲ μετρίως ἔχειν καὶ
25 φιλανθρώπως. τοιοῦτος γὰρ ὢν παρὰ τῶν ὄχλων τὴν εὐφημίαν καὶ
τὴν ἀρχὴν ἀσάλευτον ἕξεις.
[12] Ὁ δὲ ἀξιωματικός ἐστιν ἐν δεήσει κείμενος καὶ ταῖς λιταῖς καὶ
ταῖς καλουμέναις λιτανείαις. κεῖται δὲ μετὰ παραιτήσεως ἐνίοτε.
οὕτως·
30 Ἐπιτετίμηκα τῷ δεῖνι περὶ ὧν ἔφης αὐτὸν εἰς σὲ διαπεπρᾶχθαι καὶ
πικρότερον ἢ προσῆκεν αὐτῷ διηνέχθην καὶ σχεδὸν ἤπερ σὺ ὑπὲρ
σεαυτοῦ. ἐμοὶ οὖν τὴν ἀδικίαν ἀνάθες καὶ εἰς τὸ πάλιν. σὲ γὰρ οἶδα
καὶ χρηστὸν καὶ τοῖς φίλοις χαριζόμενον. δάμασον τοίνυν καθ'
Ὅμηρον θυμὸν μέγαν, οὐδέ τί σε χρὴ νηλεὲς ἦτορ ἔχειν. στρεπτοὶ δέ
35 τε καὶ θεοὶ αὐτοί.

[8] It is the threatening type when with intensity we instill fear in people for what they have done or would do. In the following manner:

If you think that you will not have to give any account for what you are about to do, then go ahead and do it. But you will see clearly that neither by soaring to the heights nor plunging to the depths will you in any manner cause a delay in your punishment. For you would find no way by which to escape what you must suffer.

[9] It is the vituperative type when we bring to light the badness of someone's character or the offensiveness of (his) action against someone. In the following manner:

Even if I should remain silent, you would hear from others how meanly and how unworthily of their conduct So-and-so has treated those men who have been entrusted with responsibility. For it is proper to write concerning matters about which some people might not know. But it is as superfluous to write concerning matters that everybody knows about and that are being noised abroad by rumor itself, as it is to make known those things which are exposed by the very fact of their being kept secret.

[10] It is the praising type when we encourage someone and express our approval of what he has done or has proposed to do, in the following manner:

I had earlier shared in your excellent character through the letters that you wrote; now I approve of what you have done and encourage you, for it will be profitable to us both.

[11] It is the advisory type when, by offering our own judgment, we exhort (someone to) something or dissuade (him) from something. For example, in the following manner:

I have briefly indicated to you those things for which I am held in high esteem by my subjects. I know, therefore, that you, too, by this course of action can gain the goodwill of your obedient subjects. Yet, while you cannot make many friends, you can be fair and humane to all. For if you are such a person, you will have a good reputation and your position will be secure among the masses.

[12] The supplicatory type consists of requests, supplications and so-called entreaties; sometimes it consists of a petition. In the following manner:

I have censured So-and-so for what you said he had done to you, and I inveighed against him more bitterly than was fitting—even more, I dare say, than you (would have done) on your own behalf. Please forgive me again, therefore, for that offense. For I know that you are good and gracious to your friends. "Gain mastery," then, as Homer says, "over your great anger; it is not at all necessary that you have a pitiless heart, for the gods themselves can be appeased." (*Iliad* 9. 496f.)

[13] Ἐρωτηματικός, ὅταν περί τινος πυνθανόμενοι παρακαλῶμεν ἡμῖν ἀντιφωνῆσαι. οἷον·
Ἀκούω τὸν δεῖνα ἐπιδεδημηκέναι πρὸς σέ. διασάφησον οὖν μοι πότερον ἔτι πάρεστιν ἢ κεχώρισται.

[14] Ἀποφαντικός ἐστι τὸ πρὸς τὸν πυνθανόμενον ἀποφαίνεσθαι. οἷον·
Ἔγραψάς μοι πυνθανόμενος εἰ παρ' ἡμῖν ὁ δεῖνα. πάρεστιν οὖν ἔτι καὶ σὲ προσδεχόμενος ἐπιμενεῖν φησιν.

[15] Ἀλληγορικός, ὅταν πρὸς ὃν γράφομεν αὐτὸν βουλώμεθα μόνον εἰδέναι καὶ δι' ἑτέρου πράγματος ⟨ἕτερον⟩ σημαίνωμεν. οἷον·
Ἀκούω τὸν πρὸς σὲ ἀγωνισόμενον ἀθλητὴν γυμνὸν ἔξω τῶν πυλῶν ἐν σκοτεινῷ κατοικεῖν οἰκήματι. συνήδομαι οὖν, ἀκονιτὶ γὰρ κρατήσεις.—οὐ γὰρ σεσήμαγκεν ὅτι ὑπείληφεν αὐτοῦ τὸν ἀντίδικον ἀπολωλέναι;

Καὶ ἕτερος ἀπειλῶν ἔγραψεν· οὐ βούλεσθε παύσασθαι, ἕως ἂν ἴδητε τοὺς τέττιγας ἐπὶ τῶν βώλων ᾄδοντας;—δι' ἄλλου γὰρ πράγματος ἄλλο ἐσήμανεν. βούλεται γὰρ εἰπεῖν ὅτι οὐ βούλεσθε παύσασθαι, ἕως ἂν ἴδητε τὴν χώραν ὑμῶν κατεσκαμμένην; οὐ γὰρ ἂν ἄλλως οἱ τέττιγες ἐπὶ τῶν βώλων ᾄδοιεν, ἀλλ' εἰ μήτε δένδρα μήτε τοίχους ἔχοιεν.

[16] Αἰτιολογικός ἐστιν, ὅταν τὰς αἰτίας δι' ἃς οὐ γέγονεν ἢ γενήσεται ὁτιδηποτοῦν, σημαίνωμεν. οἷον·
Ἔγραψάς μοι διὰ τάχους πρὸς σὲ ἐλθεῖν, κἀμοὶ δὲ τοῦτο προέκειτο. πάντα δ' ἡμῖν τὰ πρὸς τὸν πλοῦν ἀντιπέπτωκεν. οὔτε γὰρ πλοῖόν ἐστι εὐπορῆσαι πάντων εἰλκυσμένων πρὸς τὰς λειτουργίας, κἂν εὕρωμεν τῶν ἀνέμων ἐναντιουμένων ἀπρακτεῖν ἀνάγκη. ἐν τῷ μεταξὺ δὲ καὶ εἰς κρίσιν ἐμπέπλεγμαι. ἐὰν οὖν ἅπαντα μεταπέσῃ ταῦτα, ἐκδέχου με.

[17] Κατηγορικὸς δέ ἐστιν ὁ ἐν καταιτιάσει τινῶν κείμενος παρὰ τὸ δέον ἐνηργημένων. οἷον·
Οὐχ ἡδέως μὲν ἔφερον ἀκούων τὰ κατ' ἐμοῦ λεγόμενα, ἦν γὰρ οὐ τῆς ἀξίας ἀγωγῆς, κακῶς δὲ καὶ σὺ τῷ κατ' ἐμοῦ λέγοντι σαυτὸν ἐνεχείρισας καίτοι εἰδὼς αὐτὸν καὶ διάβολον καὶ ψευδολόγον. τὸ καθόλου δὲ λυπεῖς φίλον ἔχων, ὃν ᾔδεις ἁπάντων ἐχθρόν, οὐδὲ τοῦτο δοκιμάσας, ὅτι τὸν ἄλλων κατηγοροῦντα πρὸς σὲ καὶ πρὸς ἄλλους εἰκὸς τοῦτο ποιεῖν κατὰ σοῦ. μέμφομαι οὖν ἐκείνῳ μὲν ὅτι ταῦτα πράττει, σοὶ δὲ ὅτι δοκῶν φρονεῖν οὐκ ἔχεις κρίσιν ὑπὲρ φίλων.

[13] It is the inquiring type when we inquire about something and urge that a reply be sent to us. For example:

I hear that So-and-so has been staying with you. Please let me know, therefore, whether he is still there or whether he has left.

[14] The responding type responds to the person making an inquiry. For example:

You wrote me asking whether So-and-so was with us. He still is, and furthermore says that he expects to wait until you arrive.

[15] It is the allegorical type when we wish the person to whom we write to be the only one to understand (what we mean), and when we intimate one thing by means of something else. For example:

I hear that the stripped athlete who would contend with you lives outside the city in a dark dwelling-place. I rejoice with you, for you will prevail without any effort.—For has he not intimated that he understood that his adversary had lost?

And someone else wrote threateningly, "Will you not stop until you see the grasshoppers singing on the ground?"—For he intimated one thing by means of another. For he wishes to say, "Will you not stop until you see your land utterly destroyed?" For the grasshoppers would sing on the ground for no other reason than that they had neither trees nor walls (to sing on).

[16] It is the accounting type when we give the reasons why something has not taken place or will not take place. For example:

You wrote to me to come to you quickly, and I intended to do so. But all circumstances have been adverse to our taking ship. For of all the ships in public service, not a single one is available. And, even if we should find one, we are forced to do nothing about it, since the winds are against us. In the meantime, I have become involved in a lawsuit. Consequently, if all these things should change, expect me.

[17] The accusing type is that which consists of an accusation of things that have been done beyond the bounds of propriety. For example:

It was not pleasant for me to hear what was being said against me, for it was at variance with my upright conduct. On the other hand, you, too, conducted yourself badly when you placed yourself in the hands of the man who was speaking against me, even though you knew him to be a slanderer and liar. Speaking in general, you continue to cause (me) grief, for you have as friend someone whom you know to be an enemy of all men. Nor have you weighed this one fact, that the man who brings accusations against (absent) people while he is with you and others, is likely to do the same thing against you. Him, therefore, I blame because he does this, but you (I blame) because, although you seem to be intelligent, you nevertheless have no discrimination with regard to the friends you keep.

[18] Ἀπολογητικὸς δέ ἐστιν ὁ πρὸς τὰ κατηγορούμενα τοὺς ἐναντίους λόγους μετ' ἀποδείξεως εἰσφέρων. οἷον·

Καλῶς ἐποίησεν ἡ τύχη μεγάλα μοι πρὸς τὴν ἀπόδειξιν περιποιήσασα. κατὰ γὰρ οὓς χρόνους φασὶ τοῦτο πεποιηκέναι με, καταπλεύσας ἤμην εἰς Ἀλεξάνδρειαν, ὥστε οὔτε συνέβη μοι ἰδεῖν οὔτε συντυχεῖν τὸν περὶ οὗ κατηγοροῦμαι. ἄλογον δὲ καὶ τὸ μηδεμιᾶς γενομένης μοι πρὸς σὲ διαφορᾶς κατηγορεῖν σου τοῦ μηδὲν ἀδικοῦντος. ἀλλὰ φαίνονται οἱ διαβαλόντες αὐτοὶ πεπραχότες τι ἄτοπον καὶ ὑποψίαν ἔχοντες μή τί σοι περὶ αὐτῶν γράψω, προδιαβεβλήκασιν ἐμέ. σὺ δὲ εἰ μὲν κεναῖς φάσεσι πεπίστευκας, εἰπέ· εἰ δὲ διαμένεις οἷον δεῖ πρὸς ἐμέ, παραγενηθέντος μου μαθήσῃ πάντα. καὶ γὰρ εἰ μὲν κατ' ἄλλων πρὸς σὲ πώποτε εἴρηκα, πιστὸν ἦν ὅτι καὶ κατὰ σοῦ πρὸς ἑτέρους. προσδέχου με οὖν καὶ πάντα πρὸς ἔλεγχον ἐλεύσεται, ἵνα σὺ μὲν γνῷς ὡς καλῶς με κέκρικας φίλον, ἐγὼ δὲ σοῦ πεῖραν ἔργῳ λάβω. σχεδὸν γὰρ οἱ διαβαλόντες ἡμᾶς μᾶλλον ἀλλήλοις προσάξουσιν καὶ ἑαυτοὺς ἀποπνίξουσιν.

[19] Συγχαρητικὸς δέ ἐστιν, ὅταν ἐπὶ μεγάλοις τισὶ καὶ παραδόξοις πράγμασι γεγονόσι περί τινα συνηδόμενοι γράφωμεν. οἷον·

Οὐχ ὑπείληφα περὶ σὲ τὸν τοῦ πράγματος κύριον γεγονέναι τοσαύτην χαρὰν ἡλίκην περὶ ἐμὲ πυθόμενον τὰ συμβεβηκότα σοι ἀγαθά. πέποιθα δὲ βουλομένης τῆς τύχης καὶ ἔτι μείζονα γενήσεσθαι. τὸ γὰρ σὸν ἦθος οὐδὲ παρὰ θεοῖς ἀπαρασήμαντόν ἐστι, δι' ἣν ἔχεις πρὸς μὲν ἀνθρώπους ἀπάντησιν, πρὸς δὲ θεοὺς εὐσέβειαν.

[20] Εἰρωνικὸς δέ ἐστιν, ὅταν ἐναντίοις πράγμασιν ἐναντία λέγωμεν καὶ τοὺς κακοὺς καλοὺς καὶ ἀγαθοὺς λέγωμεν. οἷον·

Ἀπέδειξας τὴν πρὸς ἡμᾶς εὔνοιαν, ἣν ἐκ πάλαι εἶχες. οὐ γὰρ λέληθεν ἡ καλὴ κἀγαθή σου προαίρεσις, διότι τὸ κατὰ σαυτὸν μέρος ἀνῄρηκας ἡμᾶς. ἐὰν δὲ τῶν ἴσων τυγχάνῃς, μὴ δυσφορήσῃς. πεπείσμεθα γάρ, ἐὰν οἱ θεοὶ θέλωσι, καιρὸν ἕξειν, οἷον αὐτὸς εὑρήσεις καθ' ἡμῶν οὐδέποτε.

[21] Ἀπευχαριστικός ἐστιν τὸ μνημονεύειν ὀφείλειν χάριν. οἷον·

Ἐφ' οἷς εὐεργέτησάς με διὰ λόγων, σπουδάσω ἔργῳ δεῖξαι τὴν ἐμαυτοῦ προαίρεσιν, ἣν ἔχω πρὸς σέ. ἔλαττον γὰρ τοῦ καθήκοντος ὑπείληφα τὸ δι' ἐμοῦ σοι γινόμενον, οὐδὲ γὰρ τὸν βίον ὑπὲρ σοῦ προέμενος ἀξίαν ἀποδώσειν χάριν ὧν εὖ πέπονθα. τῶν κατ' ἐμὲ δὲ ὅ τι βούλει, μὴ γράφε παρακαλῶν, ἀλλ' ἀπαιτῶν χάριν. ὀφείλω γάρ.

[18] The apologetic type is that which adduces, with proof, arguments which contradict charges that are being made. For example:

Fortune has served me well by preserving for me important facts to be used in the demonstration of my case. For at the time that they say I did this, I had already sailed for Alexandria, so that I happened neither to see nor meet the person about whom I am accused. Since there has been no disagreement between you and me, it is absurd for you to accuse someone who has wronged you in no way. But those who brought the accusation appear themselves to have perpetrated some foul deed, and, suspecting that I might write you something about them, they (took care) to slander me in anticipation. If you have believed their empty accusations, tell me. On the other hand, if you persevere with me as you should, you will learn everything when I arrive. In fact, one could be confident that, if I had at any time spoken against other people to you, I would also have spoken against you to others. So, wait for my arrival, and everything will be put to the proof, so that you may know how rightly you have judged me to be your friend, and I may prove you by your actions. I dare say that those who accused us will rather attack each other and choke themselves.

[19] It is the congratulatory type when we write and rejoice with someone over the important and wonderful things that have happened to him. For example:

I did not realize that you had become a person of such consequence, and that you would be so delighted at my inquiring about the good things that have happened to you. But I am confident, Fortune willing, that you will become even greater. For your character has not escaped the notice of the gods. To it you owe the reception you meet with among men and your piety toward the gods.

[20] It is the ironic type when we speak of things in terms that are their opposites, and when we call bad men noble and good. For example:

You have (now) shown the goodwill toward us that you have had for a long time. For your noble and good policy (toward us) has not gone unnoticed, since, as far as you are concerned, you have ruined us. But if you should get what you deserve, do not be distressed, for we are confident, the gods willing, that we shall have such an opportunity (to repay you) as you will never have against us.

[21] The thankful type calls to mind the gratitude that is due (the reader). For example:

I hasten to show in my actions how grateful I am to you for the kindness you showed me in your words. For I know that what I am doing for you is less than I should, for even if I gave my life for you, I should still not be giving adequate thanks for the benefits I have received. If you wish anything that is mine, do not write and request it, but demand a return. For I am in your debt.

Philostratus of Lemnos

De Epistulis (II 257, 29–258, 28 Kayser)*

Τὸν ἐπιστολικὸν χαρακτῆρα τοῦ λόγου μετὰ τοὺς παλαιοὺς ἄριστά
μοι δοκοῦσι διεσκέφθαι φιλοσόφων μὲν ὁ Τυανεὺς καὶ Δίων,
στρατηγῶν δὲ Βροῦτος ἢ ὅτῳ Βροῦτος ἐς τὸ ἐπιστέλλειν ἐχρῆτο, βασι-
5 λέων δὲ ὁ θεσπέσιος Μάρκος ἐν οἷς ἐπέστελλεν αὐτός, πρὸς γὰρ τῷ
κεκριμένῳ τοῦ λόγου καὶ τὸ ἑδραῖον τοῦ ἤθους ἐντετύπωτο τοῖς γράμμασι, ῥητόρων δὲ ἄριστα μὲν Ἡρώδης ὁ Ἀθηναῖος ἐπέστελλεν, ὑπερ-
αττικίζων δὲ καὶ ὑπερλαλῶν ἐκπίπτει πολλαχοῦ τοῦ πρέποντος ἐπιστολῇ χαρακτῆρος. δεῖ γὰρ φαίνεσθαι τῶν ἐπιστολῶν τὴν ἰδέαν
10 ἀττικωτέραν μὲν συνηθείας, συνηθεστέραν δὲ ἀττικίσεως καὶ συγ-
κεῖσθαι μὲν πολιτικῶς, τοῦ δὲ ἁβροῦ μὴ ἀπάδειν. ἐχέτω δὲ τὸ
εὔσχημον ἐν τῷ μὴ ἐσχηματίσθαι, εἰ γὰρ σχηματιοῦμεν, φιλοτιμεῖσθαι
δόξομεν, φιλοτιμία δὲ ἐν ἐπιστολῇ μειρακιῶδες. κύκλον δὲ ἀποτορ-
νεύειν ἐν μὲν ταῖς βραχυτέραις τῶν ἐπιστολῶν ξυγχωρῶ, ἵνα τούτῳ
15 γοῦν ἡ βραχυλογία ὡραίζοιτο ἐς ἄλλην ἠχὼ πᾶσα στενὴ οὖσα, τῶν δὲ
ἐς μῆκος προηγμένων ἐπιστολῶν ἐξαιρεῖν χρὴ κύκλους, ἀγωνιστι-
κώτερον γὰρ ἢ κατὰ ἐπιστολὴν τοῦτο, πλὴν εἰ μή που ἐπὶ τελευτῆς
τῶν ἐπεσταλμένων ἢ ξυλλαβεῖν δέοι τὰ προειρημένα ἢ ξυγκλεῖσαι τὸ
ἐπὶ πᾶσι νόημα. σαφήνεια δὲ ἀγαθὴ μὲν ἡγεμών ἅπαντος λόγου, μά-
20 λιστα δὲ ἐπιστολῆς. καὶ γὰρ διδόντες καὶ δεόμενοι καὶ ξυγχωροῦντες
καὶ μὴ καὶ καθαπτόμενοι καὶ ἀπολογούμενοι καὶ ἐρῶντες ῥᾷον πεί-
σομεν, ἢν σαφῶς ἑρμηνεύσωμεν· σαφῶς δὲ ἑρμηνεύσομεν καὶ ἔξω
εὐτελείας, ἢν τῶν νοηθέντων τὰ μὲν κοινὰ καινῶς φράσωμεν, τὰ δὲ
καινὰ κοινῶς.

---

*Text: *Flavii Philostrati Opera*. Ed. by C. L. Kayser (Leipzig: Teubner, 1871). Vol. 2.

Philostratus of Lemnos

On Letters   *(third century A. D.)*

Those who, next to the ancients, seem to me to have used the epistolary style of discourse best are, of the philosophers (Apollonius) of Tyana and Dio, of military commanders Brutus or the person Brutus employed to write his letters, of the Emperors the divine Marcus when he himself wrote (for in addition to his distinction in speech, his firmness of character, too, had been imprinted in his letters). Of the rhetoricians Herodes the Athenian was the best at writing letters although he does, through excessive Atticism and loquacity, in many places depart from the appropriate epistolary style. For the epistolary style must in appearance be more Attic than everyday speech, but more ordinary than Atticism, and it must be composed in accordance with common usage, yet not be at variance with a graceful style. It should be graceful without making covert allusions, for if we make covert allusions we shall appear to be ambitious, and ambition in a letter is puerility. I agree to rounding off a period in shorter letters in order that in this way, at least, their brevity, in all its conciseness, may assume the beauty of a different sort of resonance. But periods must be eliminated from letters that run to any length, for this is too rhetorically impressive for an epistle, with the exception that they may possibly be used, if there be need, at the end of what has been written, either to pull together what has been said or finally to conclude the thought. While clarity is a good guide for all discourse, it is especially so for a letter. Whether we grant something or make a petition, whether we agree or disagree, whether we attack someone or defend ourselves, or whether we state our love, we shall more easily prevail if we express ourselves with clarity of style. We shall express ourselves clearly and without vulgarity if we express some of our ordinary thoughts in a novel manner, and some novel thoughts in a familiar manner.

43

Papyrus Bononiensis 5*

	I.		II.
1	ingratum]		ἀχάριστον
2	sentiet]		αἰσθήσεται
3	aut uel]ut . in . ertes . nos		ἢ ὡς ἀδρανῶν ἡμῶν
5 4	sit expe]rtus		πεῖραν λάβῃ

	I.	II.
5	Grate tibi]	Ἡδέως σοι
6	esse obsecutum]	παρηκολουθηκέναι
7	commendati]oni meae	τῆς ἐμῆς συστάσεως
8	mi frater grat]ulor	ἄδελφε συνχαίρω
10 9	in expli]cationem	ἐν τῇ ἐκπλοκῇ
10	Quinti]	Κοίντου
11	hanc rem]	οὗτο πρᾶγμα
12	quo modo]	ὡδηποτοῦν τρόπω
13	te decuit]	ἀπό σου ἔπρεπεν
15 14	explicatam] *esse didici*	ἐκπεπλεγμένον ἔμαθον
15	set et uerec]undia[e] tuae	ἀλλὰ καὶ ἡ αἰδημοσύνη ἡ σὴ
16	et continentia]e	καὶ ἐνκράτεια
17	laetor]	τέρπομαι
18	quod ingen]ium tuum	ἀτοῖς ἤθεσι σου
20 19	ita me rem]uneratur	ἀνταμειψαμένου ἡμᾶς
20	habeo]	ἔχω
21	ingratum]	τὸν ἀχάριστον
22	quid ergo es]t	τί οὖν ἐστιν
23	spero ut bre]ui . tibi	ἐλπίζω ἐν ταχεῖ σοι
25 24	huius deb]iti . tui	τούτου τοῦ ὀφλήματος
25	sim compu]tator	γενέσθαι σοι σύλλογος

| 26 |] | [de minimi]s legatis |

| 27 |]suasor[i]ae | |

*Text: *Papyri Bononienses* (P. Bon.), Ed. O. Montevecchi. (Pubb. dell' Univ. Cattolica del sacro cuore, N.S. 42; Milan: Vitae a Pensiero, 1953). Vol. 1. Trans. Benjamin Fiore, S. J.

Bologna Papyrus 5 *(third or fourth century A. D.)*

I 1–4 [He will think
it ungrateful.] [Or]
he [would pro]ve us
to be idlers.

II 1–4 He will see
it as ungrateful, or
would prove us to be
idlers.

(Congratulatory Letter)

I 5–25 [with pleas-
ure] I congratulate
[you], [my brother],
[for having followed
my recommenda]tions
[in the expo]sure [of
Quintus]. I heard
[that this matter was
expedited and how it
befit you]. [And I
am happy] at both
your [mod]esty [and
self-control],
[because in this way]
your [natural ta]lent
[rep]ays [me]. [But I
have an (outstanding)
debt. What, then is
it?] [I hope that I
might] soon [give]
you [an accounting of
this obligation] of
yours.

II 5–25 Happily
brother, do I con-
gratulate you for
having paid close
attention to my re-
commendation in the
exposure of Quintus.
I heard that this
matter was expedited

and
how it was quite wor-
thy of you. But, oh,
your modesty and
self-control! I
delight in your very
character, since in
this you repaid us.
I have an (outstand-
ing) debt. What,
then, is it? I hope
soon to [give] you
an accounting of
this obligation of
yours.

I II 26–27 (Letters) of Advice [about Very Small] Legacies

45

	III.	IV.
1	συνβουλευτικαὶ περὶ ἐλαχίστων	
2	καταλελειμμεων	
3	Lic[i]nn[i]um amicum tibi	Λικίννιον φίλον σου
4	ue]rum	γνήσιον
5	*obitum* com . pertus sum	τεθνηκότα ἔμαθον
6	q]uem *parum* memorem	ὃν ὀλίγον ἐμνημονευ[κό]τα
7	ob . *sequi* . *tui* [*fu*]*isse*	τῆς σῆς ὑπεικίας γεγο[νέ]ν̣α̣ι
8	doleo . *quidem*	λυποῦμαι μὲν
9	s[*et hortor te*	ἀλλὰ παρορμῶ σε
10	u]*t fortiter fe*ras	εὐσταθῶς ἐνεγκεῖ̣ν̣
11	t]*abulas enim* suppremorum	διαθήκας μὲν γὰρ ἐσχάτων
12	h]omin[e]*s quid*em faciunt	ἄνθρωποι μέν ποιοῦσιν̣
13	s]et ordinant fata	διατάσσουσιν δὲ μοῖρα[ι]
14	Quod al*iter*	Ὅπερ ἄλλως
15	quam meruisse . te	ἢ ἠξιῶσθαί σε
16	s]cimus	οἴδαμεν
17	remuneratus . non . es	οὐκ ἀντεδωρήθη[ς]
18	a . Publio *a*mico . tuo	ἀπὸ Πουβλίου τοῦ φί̣λ̣ου σου
19	quem defunctum	ὃν τεθνηκότα
20	n]aran*t* . litterae	λέγουσιν τὰ γράμματα
21	nihil e*x* moribus tuis	μηδὲν οὖν ἐκ τῶν σῶν
22	cum . et	ἀλλαξέτω
23	parum . ingrata . sententia	οὕτως ἀχάριστος ἀπόφασις
24	omnes enim homines	πάντες γὰρ ἄνθρωποι
25	*inaeq*[u]*a*[l]*es sumus*	ἄνισοί ἐσμεν

III IV 1–2 (Letters) of Advice about Very Small Legacies

III 3–13 I learned
that Lic[i]nn[i]us, a
[gen]uine friend of
yours, has died.
And, to be sure, I am
unhappy that he [w]as
so little mindful of
your loyalty. [B]ut
I urge you to bear it
with resolution.
For, really, [p]eople
draw up [w]ills for
their final deposi-
tions, [b]ut the
fates dispose of
them.

IV 3–13 I heard that
Licinnius has died, a
genuine friend of
yours, but one who
little remembered
your allegiance.
I am sorry, but I
urge you to bear it
calmly. For while
people draw up wills
for their final depo-
sitions, the fates
dispose of them.

III 14–25 We [k]now
that you were not
repaid by Publius,
your friend, which is
not at all what you
deserved. The docu-
ments describe the
deceased, (but say)
nothing about your
character since this
is so very ungrateful
a decision. Indeed,
all of us men are
uneq[u]a[l].

IV 14–25 We know that
[your] gifts were not
matched by Publius,
which is not at all
what you deserved.
The documents (only)
describe the
deceased. Do not,
then, let so ungra-
cious an omission
take away anything
from what is yours.
Indeed, all of us men
are unequal.

26   Parum grate *in meri*ta *tua*   Ὠλιγωρηκέγαι τὴν σὴν
                                                        παρ[οχὴν

	V.		VI.

1   *in* [sup]*premis suis*   ἐν τοῖς ἐσχά[το]ις αὐτοῦ
2   *Licinnium ami*cum   Λικίννιον τὸν φίλον
3   q]uondam *commune*m   ποτὲ κοινὸν
4   m]irar]er quidem   ἐθαύμαζον ἂν
5   n]isi . [put]*arem*   εἰ μὴ συνελογιζόμην
6   *tam* [prosp]era *re*[s]   τὰ κρείττονα
7   qu]am a[du]*ersa*[s]   ἢ τὰ φαῦλα
8   qua*ec*[umque mort]*alibu*[s]   ἅτινα θνητοῖς
9   *adsc*[riptae] sunt   τροσγέγραπται
10   non . e[sse]   μὴ εἶναι
11   i]*n* tua [potest]*a*[te]   ἐν τῇ σῇ ἐξουσίᾳ

12   gr]*atulato*[ri]*ae* hereditatum acceptarum

                        συνχ]αριστ[ι]καὶ κληρονομιῶν καταλελειμ(μένων)
13   ἐ]π[ι]στ[ο]λαί
14

15   *M*[e]*ritissimo tibi*   Ἀξιωτάτῳ σοι
16   fr*ater*   ἄδελφε
17   *heredi*tatem   κληρονομίαν
18   cum summo [honor]e   μετὰ μεγάλης τειμῆς
19   accessis]*se* gra[tulo]*r*   προσεληλυθέναι συνχαίρω
20   *et* iu*dicium*   καὶ τὴν κρίσιν
21   *amicorum* tuorum   τῶν σῶν φίλων
22   u]*sque* [ad] supprem[am   ἕως τῆς ἐσχάτης
23   s]uime[t] memoria*m*   ἑαυτῶν μνήμης
24   ob . sequis . tuis   ταῖς σαῖς παρακολουθίαις
25   grate . respondere   ἡδέως ὑπακούειν
26   laetor   χαίρω

(Ironic Letter? Letter of Reproach?)

III 26–V 11 [I would
really] be [a]mazed
that Licinnius,
[o]nce a mutual
friend, decided
things in his will
with too little
thanks in relation to
what you deserve, if
I did not [think]
that [prosper]ity no
less than
a[dv]ersity,
whiche[ver one] is
de[signated] for
[mort]als, i[s] not
under your
[contr]o[l].

IV 26–VI 11 I would
be amazed that Licin-
nius, once a mutual
friend, had taken
slight account of
your gen[erosity] in
his las[t] will, if I
did not come to the
conclusion that
advantages or sorry
circumstances, which-
ever are designated
to mortals, are not
under your control.

V VI 12 [Cong]ratulat[or]y (Letters) for Inheritances Received

V VI 13–14 [Cong]ratulatory [L]et[t]ers for Bequeat[hed] Inheritances

V 15–26 Brother, I
congra[tul]ate you
that an inheritance
with great [honor]
has [come] to you,
who most deserve it.
And I am happy that
the judgment of your
friends offers a
return in thanks for
your services (to
them), right up [to]
[t]heir final remem-
brance.

VI 15–26 Brother, I
congratulate you that
an inheritance with
great honor has come
to you who most
deserve it. And I am
happy that the judg-
ment of your friends
is pleased to take
heed of your service
(to them), right up
to their final remem-
brance.

27	*Quam . quam tibi*		Καὶ ε̣ἰ̣ μ̣ὲ̣ν̣ [ἔδει σε
28	*hereditate accepta*		κλη̣ϱονομ̣[ίαν δεξάμ]ενον
29	*gratulari fas*		χαίϱειν
30	*tamen uni tibi*		]ε̣ σο̣ι̣

		VII.		VIII.
	I	*n*[on] audeo		οὐ θαϱϱῶ
	2	noui . enim		οἶδα γὰϱ
	3	an[i]mi tui . propositum		τῆς ψυχῆς σου [τὸ] προκείμενον
10	4	cum numquam par . est		ἢ οὐδέποτε ἴσ̣[η ἐσ]τὶ̣ν̣
	5	desiderio . amici		ἐπιθυμία φίλο[υ]
	6	e[*x* iudicio . eius		ἐκ τῆς αὐτοῦ [κρίσ]εως
	7	so]lacium . fit		παραμυθία γε[ίνε]τ̣α̣ι̣
	8	*Mu*[lt]*u*m tibi . frater		Πολύ σοι ἄδελφε
15	9	*pro*ficere . reuerentiam		προκόπτειν [τὴν εὐσέβειαν]
	10	*q*[u]*a* semper amicos		ἢν ἀεὶ φίλοις
	11	intueris		παρέχῃ
	12	*et p*lenissima		καὶ πληϱεστάτ[η]
	13	[u]ene[*r*]*a*tione		ἐπαφϱεδεισία (sic)
20	14	c]onseruas		συντηϱεῖς
	15	memoriam		μνήμην
	16	R]utili . amici		Ῥουτιλίου φίλου
	17	aliquando commun[i]*s*		ποτὲ κοινοῦ
	18	s]um . expertus		ἐπ[ει]ϱάθην
25	19	*q*]ui . etiam . uidebatur		ὃς καὶ φανεϱὸς
	20	non . exiguo . numero		οὐκ ἐν ἐλαχίστῳ [ἀριθμῷ
	21	p[ropinquorum . relicto		ἀγ[χ]ιστέων κατ[αλελειμμένῳ
	22	processerit		προβεβηκὼς
	23	parte tamen te		μέϱος μέντοι γά[ϱ] σε
30	24	non *minima*		οὐκ ἐλάχιστον
	25	*h*ereditatis		κληϱονομίας
	26	una] c[um] suis		σὺν τοῖς ἰδίοις
	27	d]*ignum iudic*aui[t]		ἄξιον ἔκϱειν[ε

V 27–VII 7 Although
it is proper to con-
gratulate you on the
reception of an
inheritance, never-
theless, in your case
alone I do [n]ot ven-
ture to do so. For I
know the purpose of
your heart. Since it
is never equal to the
desire of a friend,
(your) [con]solation
comes in consequence
of his decision in
the will.

VI 27–VIII 7 Although
[one ought to have]
rejoiced at your
[receiv]ing an inher-
itance, nonetheless,
in your case (alone)
I do not venture to
do so. For I know
the purpose of your
heart, to which the
desire [of] your
friend i[s] never
equal. (Your) conso-
lation (must there-
fore) derive from his
[deci]sion in the
will.

VII 8–27 Brother, the
respect with which
you always regard
your friends brings
you
[gr]eat profit. And
with the highest
[e]steem you
[pr]eserve the memory
of [R]utilius, once a
mutual friend. I know
the man full well,
[w]ho, when he passed
away, was conspicuous
for the large number
of his surviving
[r]elatives. Never-
theless, he judged
you [w]orthy of an
appreciable part of
the inheritance,
[along] w[ith] the
rest of his own kin.

VIII 8–27 Brother,
[the respect] which
you always show your
friends brings you
great
prosperity. And with
the greatest charm
you preserve the mem-
ory of Rutilius, once
a mutual friend. I
know the man full
well, who, although
he passed away con-
spicuous for the
large [number] of his
sur[viving] relatives,
nonetheless judged
you worthy of an
appreciable part of
the inheritance,
along with his own
kin.

	28	T . . . m . [ ]*do*mine	Τει [ ]τ....α..λ..μο
	29	tuor[u]m [obsequiorum]	τῶ]γ σῷγ [ὑπουργιῶν
		IX.	X.

		*fuis*se	γε[γενῆσθαι
5	2	in] supprem[is s]uis	[ἐν] τ[οῖς ἐσχάτο]ις αὐτοῦ
	3	L[i]cinium	Λ[ικ]ί[ννιον
	4	g[r]atulor . tibi	συνχαίρω σοι
	5	set . et . eis . pariter	ἀλλὰ καὶ ἐκείνοις ὁμόσε
	6	quos . amas	οὓς φιλεῖς
10	7	*idest* nobis	τουτέστιν ἡμεῖν
	8	quando . enim	[ὁπό]τε γὰρ
	9	obsequ*ia tua*	αἱ σαὶ ὑπουργίαι
	10	remun[e]*rantur*	ἀντιδωροῦνται
	11	omnes	πά[ν]τες
15	12	per . processorum . tuo*rum*	ἐν [τ]α[ῖ]ς σαῖς προκοπαῖς
	13	clientes . tui	οἱ π[ροσήκον]τες σου
	14	augentur	αὐ[ξάν]ουσιν

	15	Memoriae . Sulpici	Μνήμη Σουλπικίου
	16	auctum . te	ηὐ[ξη]μένον σε
20	17	pauperis . quidem	με[τ]ρίου [μ]ὲν
	18	set amici . tui	ἀλλ[ά] σου φίλου
	19	gaudeo	χ[αίρ]ω
	20	*quod . uolun*tas . eius	διόπερ ἡ κρίσις αὐτοῦ
	21	praesta*nti*am tuam	τὴν σὴν παροχὴν
25	22	sic remunerauit	οὕτως ἀνταμείψατο
	23	ut int[elle]gi possit	ἵνα αἰσθάνεσθαι δύνηται
	24	eum ti[bi]	τοῦτόν σοι
	25	quod . *tantum* . quod . boluit	οὐ μόνον τὸ ἠθέλησεν
	26	set *quod pot*uit	ἀλλὰ ὃ ἠδυνήθη
30	27	reliquis*se*	καταλέλοιπεν
	28	diu*turn*us enim languor	μακρονοσία γὰρ
	29	et senec[ta]	καὶ γῆρας

| | | XI. | XII. |

	1	quae sa]epe etiam	ὃ πολλὰ]κις
35	2	langu]ore deterior . est	καὶ] νόσου χεῖρόν ἐστιν
	3	uniu]ersam	συ]νάπασαν
	4	sub]stantiam . eius	τὴ]ν ὑπόστασιν αὐτοῦ
	5	ab . sum . pserat	ἀνηλώκει

VII 28–IX 14 I
[con]gratulate you,
Sir, that L[i]cinnius
was [_____] of
your [services in
h]is last will. But
I am likewise happy
for those of us as
well whom you regard
as friends. For when
your services are
repaid, all your
dependents are
enriched through your
prosperity.

VIII 28–X 14 I con-
gratulate you, Sir,
that L[ic]innius]
w[as] [_____] of
your [services in]
his [last will]. But
I am likewise happy
for those of us as
well whom you regard
as friends. For
[wh]en your services
are repaid, al[l]
your a[ssocia]tes
g[r]ow in prosperity.

IX 15–XI 5 I am
happy that you have
been enriched by the
remembrance in Sulpi-
cius's will, a man of
modest means, but
your friend. His
will repaid your ser-
vice in this manner
in order that he
might be understood
by you. He left you
not only what he
wanted to, but what
he was able to. For
long-lasting physical
ailment and old age,
[which is of]ten
worse than [phy]sical
disability, consumed
his entire substance.

X 15–XII 5 I am
h[app]y that you have
been en[ri]ched by
the remembrance in
Sulpicius's
will, a man of
mo[d]est means, but
your friend. His
decision repaid your
service in this man-
ner in order to make
himself clear to you.
He left you not only
what he wanted to,
but what he was able
to. For lingering
illness and old age,
[often] [even] worse
than sickness, con-
sumed his entire sub-
stance.

	6	Honesto . titulo te	Εὐσχήμονι ἐλέγχῳ σε
	7	*Fab*iani amici tui	Φαβιανοῦ φίλου σου
	8	*ob*iti honoratum	ἀποθανόντος ἠξιῶσθαι με
			χαίρω
5	9	*qua*m . quam . tu	ὅπερ σὺ
	10	m]oleste . feras	ἀναξιοπαθεῖς
	11	eg]o tamen	ἐγὼ μέντοι
	13	*d*[u]pliciter . gaudeo	δισσῶς ἱλαρός εἰμι
	13	qu]od . et . iudicia . eius	ὅτι καὶ ἡ κρίσις αὐ[τ]οῦ
10	14	qualis . in . eum . fue*ris*	ὁποῖον εἰς [α]ὐτ[ὸ]ν γέγονας
	15	os]*t*endunt	ἐπιδείκνυ[σι]ν
	16	*et* . quod. ca*ndoris*	καὶ τῆς λα[μπ]ρότ[η]τος
	17	*ani*mi tui	τῆς ψυχῆς [σου]
	18	am]*p*[*l*]*iament*[u]*m*	ἐπειφόρη[μ]αι
15	19	li]*beralitatis*	ἐ]λευθεριότητος
	20	*accessit*	π]ροσῆλθεν
	21	s]uadeo . ergo	συ]νβουλεύω τοιγαροῦν
	22	dolori desinas	παύεσθαι πονῶν
	23	amicus enim	φίλος γὰρ
20	24	qui ita] testatur	ὃς οὕτως διατίθη[σιν
	25	non] lacrimis	οὐ δάκρυσιν
	26	set] animo	ἀλλὰ ψυχῇ
	27	*desi*derandus [est]	ἐπιζητητέος ἐ[στίν]

(A Letter of Mixed Type: Congratulation and Advice?)

XI 6–27 You were
honored with the
token of your
deceased friend
Fabianus's respect,
although you lamented
his loss. Nonethe-
less, I am doubly
glad, both that the
determinations of his
will show what you
meant to him, and
that, because of your
magnanimity an
increase of generos-
ity came to you.
Therefore, I advise
you to end your
grieving. For a
friend who makes
[such] a will [is] to
be missed [not] by
tears [but] in one's
heart.

XII 6–27 I am
delighted that when
your friend Fabianus
died, you
received a noble
proof of your worth,
although you suffered
undeserved pain.
Nevertheless I am
doubly glad, both
that his will shows
what you meant to
him, and that,
because of [your]
magnanimity, an
increase of generos-
ity came to you.
Therefore, I advise
you to end your
grieving. For a
friend who makes such
a will is to be
missed not by tears
but in one's heart.

		XIII.	XIV.
	1	gratulatoria]e libertatis acceptae]	
	2		συνχαριστικαὶ]
	3	Lib]ertati quidem	Τῇ [μὲν] ἐλευθερίᾳ
5	4	o[m]nes favemus	πά]ντες σπουδάζομεν
	5	meritissimo . autem tibi	ἀ[ξι]ωτάτῳ δέ σοι
	6	contigisse . scimus	γεγενῆσθ[αι] οἴδαμεν
	7	ego [c]erte	εἰς τάδε ἐγὼ
	8	pecu[l]iariter gaudeo	καθ᾿ ἰδίαν [χαί]ρω
10	9	quod eam	ἐπειδεὰν ἀτὴν
	10	tam iudicio . domini . tui	καὶ τῇ [κ]ρίσ[ει] το[ῦ κυρίου σου]
	11	qua[m] meritis . tuis	καὶ τ[ῇ παροχῇ σου
	12	c]on[s]ecu[t]us es	ἔτυχες
15	13	sequiens est ergo	ἀκόλουθον [οὖν ἐστιν
	14	ut . perpetui . eui	ἵνα ἡ διηνεκὴς αἰὼν
	15	omni uitae tuae	πάσῃ [τῇ] ζωῇ σου
	16	spatali du[l]ci[a]	ἐπὶ πλ[εῖ]στον δοθῇ
	17	suabitatis	ἡδὺ
20	18	semina	τῇ συνκράσ[ε]ι τῶν τρόπ[ων]
	19	consequantur	τύχην ἀ[κολουθεῖ]ν
	20	his enim demum	αὕτη [γὰρ] οὕτως
	21	be]atus est	εὔμοιρός ἐστιν
	22	situlus	στήλη
25	23	ut . illud	ἵνα κεῖνος
	24	libertatis . ornamentum	τῆς ἐλευθερίας [κόσμος]
	25	constet . inter [omne]s	συνεστηκέ[ναι πᾶσιν δηλωθῇ
	26	non . datam . tib[i]	μὴ δεδομέν[ην σοι
	27	set reddita[m	ἄλλὰ ἀποδε[δομένην
	28	Semper quidem [fortuna	Πάντοτε μὲν τύχ[η

XIII XIV 1 Congratulatory Letters on the Reception of Freedom

XIII XIV 2 Congratulatory Letters

XIII 3–28 We all
cherish freedom, but
we know that it has
come to you most
deservingly. Surely,
I am particularly
glad that you have
attained it both by
the decision of your
master and by your
own merits. It fol-
lows, therefore, for
the sweet seeds of
delight to accompany
the unending span of
your whole life.
Hence there is this
happy inscription
precisely so that the
ornament of freedom
might stand manifest
in [every]one's view
for them to know that
freedom was not
granted to you but
was restored. To be
sure, fortune always
. . .

XIV 3–28 We all
cherish freedom, but
we know that it has
come to you most
deservingly. I am
particularly
[plea]sed for the
following reasons:
that you have
attained it both by
the decision of [your
master] and by [what
you yourself contrib-
uted]. It is consis-
tent with this, in
order that a very
long and most plea-
sant life be granted
you, that fortune
[follows]
the influences of the
heavenly bodies in
their movements.
[For] the inscription
(declaring your free-
dom) is so happy a
dispensation of for-
tune that that
[decoration] of free-
dom [may be disclosed
to all], not to be
something that has
been granted [to
you], but something
that has been
re[stored]. Fortune
at all times . . .

Gregory of Nazianzus

Epistula 51*

⟨Νικοβούλῳ⟩

[1] Τῶν γραφόντων ἐπιστολὰς (ἐπειδὴ καὶ τοῦτο αἰτεῖς), οἱ μὲν μακρότερα γράφουσιν ἤπερ εἰκός, οἱ δὲ καὶ λίαν ἐνδεέστερα· καὶ ἀμφό-
τεροι τοῦ μετρίου διαμαρτάνουσιν, ὥσπερ τῶν σκοπῶν οἱ τοξεύοντες,
ἄν τε εἴσω πέμπωσιν, ἄν τε ὑπερπέμπωσι· τὸ γὰρ ἀποτυγχάνειν ἴσον,
κἂν ἀπὸ τῶν ἐναντίων γίνηται.
[2] Ἔστι δὲ μέτρον τῶν ἐπιστολῶν, ἡ χρεία· καὶ οὔτε μακρότερα
γραπτέον, οὗ μὴ πολλὰ τὰ πράγματα, οὔτε μικρολογητέον, ἔνθα
πολλά. [3] Τί γάρ; Ἢ τῇ περσικῇ σχοίνῳ μετρεῖσθαι δεῖ τὴν σοφίαν,
ἢ παιδικοῖς πήχεσι, καὶ οὕτως ἀτελῆ γράφειν ὡς μηδὲ γράφειν, ἀλλὰ
μιμεῖσθαι τῶν σκιῶν τὰς μεσημβρινὰς ἢ τῶν γραμμῶν τὰς κατὰ
πρόσωπον ἀταντώσας, ὧν συνιζάνει τὰ μήκη καὶ παραφαίνεται μᾶλλον ἢ φαίνεται τῶν ἄκρων τισὶ γνωριζόμενα, καὶ ἔστιν, ὡς ἂν εἴποιμι
καιρίως, εἰκασμάτων εἰκάσματα; Δέον, ἀμφοτέρων φεύγοντα τὴν
ἀμετρίαν, τοῦ μετρίου κατατυγχάνειν. [4] Περὶ μὲν δὴ τῆς συντομίας
ταῦτα γινώσκω·

Περὶ δὲ σαφηνείας ἐκεῖνο γνώριμον, ὅτι χρὴ φεύγοντα τὸ
λογοειδές, ὅσον ἐνδέχεται, μᾶλλον εἰς τὸ λαλικὸν ἀποκλίνειν· καί, ἵν'
εἴπω συντόμως, αὕτη τῶν ἐπιστολῶν ἀρίστη καὶ κάλλιστα ἔχουσα, ἣ
ἂν καὶ τὸν ἰδιώτην πείθῃ καὶ τὸν πεπαιδευμένον, τὸν μέν, ὡς κατὰ
τοὺς πολλοὺς οὖσα, τὸν δέ, ὡς ὑπὲρ τοὺς πολλούς, καὶ ᾗ αὐτόθεν
γνώριμος· ὁμοίως γὰρ ἄκαιρον καὶ γρῖφον νοεῖσθαι καὶ ἐπιστολὴν
ἑρμηνεύεσθαι.

*Text: *Gregor von Nazianz: Briefe.* Ed. P. Gallay (Griechische christliche Schriftsteller; Berlin: Akademie-Verlag, 1969).

Gregory of Nazianzus

Epistle 51   *(A. D. 384–390)*

(To Nicobulus)

[1] Among people who write letters (since you have also inquired about this subject) there are some who write at greater length than is fitting, and others who are much too brief. They both completely miss achieving the mean, just as archers either undershoot or overshoot when they try to hit the target. They miss equally, though for opposite reasons.

[2] What determines the length of letters is the need they aim to meet. One should not write on and on when the subject matter is limited, nor be stingy with words when there is much to say. [3] What? Must one's skill (in writing letters) be measured by the Persian schoinos or by the "children's cubits"? And should one write ineffectually to the point that it is not even writing? Should we copy the (well-defined) shadows at noon, or, on the contrary, the lines we look at from their ends — with the result that their lengths are telescoped and only a glimpse of them is caught, and they are not seen from one end to the other by anyone? They are, if I may make a timely remark, likenesses of likenesses. One should avoid the excesses of both and achieve the mean. [4] These, then, are my thoughts on conciseness.

As to clarity, everyone knows that one should avoid prose-like style so far as possible, and rather incline towards the conversational. To put it briefly, the best and most beautifully written letter is the one that is persuasive to the uneducated and educated alike, appearing to the former as written on the popular level, and to the latter as above that level, a letter which furthermore is understood at once. For it were as inopportune that a riddle be seen through (at once) as that a letter be in need of interpretation.

[5] Τρίτον ἐστὶ τῶν ἐπιστολῶν, ἡ χάρις. Ταύτην δὲ φυλάξομεν, εἰ μήτε παντάπασι ξηρὰ καὶ ἀχάριστα γράφοιμεν καὶ ἀκαλλώπιστα, ἀκόσμητα καὶ ἀκόρητα, ὃ δὴ λέγεται, οἷον δὴ γνωμῶν καὶ παροιμιῶν καὶ ἀποφθεγμάτων ἐκτός, ἔτι δὲ σκωμμάτων καὶ αἰνιγμάτων, οἷς ὁ λόγος καταγλυκαίνεται· μήτε λίαν τούτοις φαινοίμεθα καταχρώμενοι· τὸ μὲν γὰρ ἀγροῖκον, τὸ δ' ἄπληστον. [6] Καὶ τοσαῦτα τούτοις χρηστέον, ὅσα καὶ ταῖς πορφύραις ἐν τοῖς ὑφάσμασι. Τροπὰς δὲ παραδεξόμεθα μέν, ὀλίγας δέ, καὶ ταύτας οὐκ ἀναισχύντους. Ἀντίθετα δὲ καὶ πάρισα καὶ ἰσόκωλα τοῖς σοφισταῖς ἀπορρίψομεν· εἰ δέ που καὶ παραλάβοιμεν, ὡς καταπαίζοντες μᾶλλον τοῦτο ποιήσομεν ἢ σπουδάζοντες. [7] Πέρας τοῦ λόγου, ὅπερ τῶν κομψῶν τινος ἤκουσα περὶ τοῦ ἀετοῦ λέγοντος, ἡνίκα ἐκρίνοντο περὶ βασιλείας οἱ ὄρνιθες καὶ ἄλλος ἄλλως ἧκον ἑαυτοὺς κοσμήσαντες, ὅτι ἐκείνου κάλλιστον ἦν τὸ μὴ οἴεσθαι καλὸν εἶναι. Τοῦτο κἂν ταῖς ἐπιστολαῖς μάλιστα τηρητέον τὸ ἀκαλλώπιστον καὶ ὅτι ἐγγυτάτω τοῦ κατὰ φύσιν.

[8] Τοσαῦτά σοι περὶ ἐπιστολῶν, ὡς δι' ἐπιστολῆς παρ' ἡμῶν· καὶ ταῦτα ἴσως οὐ πρὸς ἡμῶν, οἷς τὰ μείζω σπουδάζεται· τἄλλα δὲ αὐτός τε φιλοπονήσεις, εὐμαθὴς ὤν, καὶ οἱ περὶ ταῦτα κομψοὶ διδάξουσιν.

[5] The third quality of a letter is its charm. This we should preserve if, on the one hand, we avoided writing with complete aridity, gracelessness and lack of embellishment, in the unadorned and untrimmed style, as it is called, which allows for no pithy sayings, proverbs or apophthegms nor for witticisms or enigmas which sweeten discourse. On the other hand we should not make undue use of these devices. Not to use them at all is boorish, to use them too much is cloying. [6] They should be used in the same way that purple threads are in robes. I consent to the use of tropes, but only a few, and they should not be in bad taste. Antitheses, parisoses and isocola I leave to the sophists, but should we somehow use them, we should do so with humor rather than seriousness. [7] I conclude my remarks with what I heard one of those clever (sophists) say: When the birds were disputing about who should be king, and they came together, each adorned in his own way, the greatest adornment of the eagle was that he did not think that he was beautiful. It is this unadorned quality, which is as close to nature as possible, that must especially be preserved in letters.

[8] Such, then, is my advice to you on the subject of letter writing—sent in the form of a letter! Perhaps you will not hold it against me, since I am busy with more important matters. As for the other aspects of letter writing, you will work hard at them yourself, since you are a fast learner, and those skilled in these matters will teach you.

Julius Victor

Ars Rhetorica 27 (De Epistolis)*

Epistolis conveniunt multa eorum, quae de sermone praecepta sunt. Epistolarum species duplex est; sunt enim aut negotiales aut familiares. Negotiales sunt argumento negotioso et gravi. In hoc genere et sententiarum pondera et
5 verborum lumina et figurarum insignia conpendii opera requiruntur atque omnia denique oratoria praecepta, una modo exceptione, ut aliquid de summis copiis detrahamus et orationem proprius sermo explicet. Si quid historicum epistola conprehenderis, declinari oportet a plena formula historiae, ne recedat ab epistolae gratia. Si quid etiam eruditius scribas, sic disputa, ut ne
10 modum epistolae corrumpas.

In familiaribus litteris primo brevitas observanda: ipsarum quoque sententiarum ne diu circumferatur, quod Cato ait, ambitio, sed ita recidantur, ut numquam verbi aliquid deesse videatur: unum 'te' scilicet, quod intellegentia suppleatur, in epistolis Tullianis ad Atticum et Axium frequentissimum est.
15 Lucem vero epistolis praefulgere oportet, nisi cum consulto [consilio] clandestinae litterae fiant, quae tamen ita ceteris occultae esse debent, ut his, ad quos mittuntur, clarae perspicuaeque sint. Solent etiam notas inter se secretiores pacisci, quod et Caesar et Augustus et Cicero et alii plerique fecerunt. Ceterum cum abscondito nihil opus est, cavenda obscuritas magis quam in
20 oratione aut in sermocinando: potes enim parum plane loquentem rogare, ut id planius dicat, quod in absen|tium epistolis non datur. Et ideo nec historia occultior addenda nec proverbium ignotius aut verbum cariosius aut figura putidior: neque dum amputatae brevitati studes, dimidiatae sententiae sit intellegentia requirenda, nec † dilatione verborum et anxio struendi labore lux
25 obruenda.

*Text: *Rhetores Latini Minores*. Ed. C. Halm (Leipzig: Teubner, 1863). Trans. Jerome Neyrey, S.J.

Julius Victor

The Art of Rhetoric 27 *(fourth century A. D.)*

On Letter Writing

Many directives which pertain to oral discourse also apply to letters. There are two kinds of letters: they are either official or personal. Official letters are such in virtue of their official and serious subject. Characteristic of this type are weighty statements, clarity of diction, and special effort at terse expression, as well as all the rules of oratory, with one exception, that we prune away some of its great size and let an appropriate familiar style govern the discourse. If you would relate a piece of history in a letter, then avoid the full procedure for (narrating) history lest it diminish the charm of the letter. If, however, you want to write something in a more learned vein, give sufficient thought not to spoil the epistolary style.

In personal letters brevity is the first norm. Do not let the display of eloquence, as Cato says, expand in all directions. On the other hand, let it be curtailed only to the point that there appears to be no omission. For example, only one "you," which the intelligent reader can supply, is more than enough in the letters of Cicero to Atticus or Axius. Clarity ought to radiate through the letters unless by design they are secret. (Which, nevertheless, ought to be cryptic to outsiders, yet perfectly evident to the intended recipients). For men are accustomed to agree on a very obscure code among themselves, as Caesar, Augustus, Cicero and other men did. When there is no need to hide anything from others, avoid obscurity more assiduously (in letters) than you do in speeches and conversation. For while you can ask someone who is speaking unclearly to elucidate his point, it is altogether impossible in correspondence when the party is absent. Therefore, do not include obscure facts of history or unknown proverbs, neither antiquated expressions nor pedantic turns of phrase. And while you strive for trenchant expression, do not be so elliptical that effort must be expended on the truncated argument: nor let clarity be obscured by verbal barrages or by turgid style.

Epistola, si superiori scribas, ne iocularis sit; si pari, ne inhumana; si inferiori, ne superba; neque docto incuriose, neque indocto indiligenter, nec coniunctissimo translatitie, nec minus familiari non amice. Rem secundam prolixius gratulare, ut illius gaudium extollas: cum offendas dolentem, pauculis consolare, quod ulcus etiam, cum plana manu tangitur, cruentatur.

Ita in litteris cum familiaribus ludes, ut tamen cogites posse evenire, ut eas litteras legant tempore tristiore. Iurgari numquam oportet, sed epistolae minime. Praefationes ac subscriptiones litterarum computandae sunt pro discrimine amicitiae aut dignitatis, habita ratione consuetudinis. Rescribere sic oportet, ut litterae, quibus respondes, prae manu sint, ne quid, cui responsio opus sit, de memoria effluat. Observabant veteres karissimis sua manu scribere vel plurimum subscribere. Commendatitias fideliter dato aut ne dato. Id fiet, si amicissime dabis ad amicissimum, et si probabile petes et si impetrabile. Graece aliquid addere litteris suave est, si id neque intempestive neque crebro facias: et proverbio uti non ignoto percommodum est, et versiculo aut parte versus.

Lepidum est nonnunquam quasi praesentem alloqui, uti 'heus tu' et 'quid ais' et 'video te deridere': | quod genus apud M. Tullium multa sunt. Sed haec, ut dixi, in familiaribus litteris; nam illarum aliarum severitas maior est. In summa id memento et ad epistolas et ad omnem scriptionem bene loqui.

A letter written to a superior should not be droll; to an equal, not cold; to an inferior, not haughty. Let not a letter to a learned person be carelessly written, nor indifferently composed when going to a less learned person; let it not be negligently written if to a close friend, nor less cordial to a non-friend. Be profuse in congratulating someone on his success so as to heighten his joy, but console someone who is grieving with a few words, for a wound bleeds when touched by a heavy hand.

When you are lighthearted in your friendly letters, reckon with the possibility that they may be reread in sadder times. Never quarrel, especially in a letter! The openings and conclusions of letters should conform with the degree of friendship (you share with the recipient) or with his rank, and should be written according to customary practice. One ought to answer letters by having at one's fingertips the very letters to which one would reply lest one forgot to what it was that he was replying. As a rule, the ancients wrote in their own hands to those closest to them, or at least frequently appended a post-script. Recommendations should be written truthfully or not at all. They are proper only when you willingly give them to a dear friend and if you make credible and realistic claims in them. It is pleasant to add a Greek phrase or two in your letter, provided it is not ill-timed or too frequent. And it is very much in form to use a familiar proverb, a line of poetry, or a snatch of verse.

Sometimes it is agreeable to write as though you were conversing with the person actually present, using expressions like "you too?" and "just as you say!" and "I see you smile . . ." which are amply found in Cicero's letters. But these expressions, as I said, pertain to personal letters, for the tone of the other types of letters must be more serious. In conclusion, be careful to discourse well both in your letters and in every other kind of writing.

Pseudo Libanius

Ἐπιστολιμαῖοι Χαρακτῆρες.*

[1] Ὁ μὲν ἐπισταλτικὸς χαρακτὴρ ποικίλος τε καὶ πολυσχιδὴς ὑπάρχει, ὅθεν τῷ γράφειν βουλομένῳ προσήκει μὴ ἁπλῶς μηδ' ὡς ἔτυχεν ἐπιστέλλειν, ἀλλὰ σὺν ἀκριβείᾳ πολλῇ καὶ τέχνῃ· ἄριστα δ' ἄν
5 τις ἐπιστεῖλαι δυνηθείη, εἰ γνοίη, τί τέ ἐστιν ἐπιστολὴ καὶ τί λέγειν ὅλως ἐν αὐτῇ θέμις καὶ εἰς πόσας προσηγορίας διαιρεῖται.

[2] Ἐπιστολὴ μὲν οὖν ἐστιν ὁμιλία τις ἐγγράμματος ἀπόντος πρὸς ἀπόντα γινομένη καὶ χρειώδη σκοπὸν ἐκπληροῦσα, ἐρεῖ δέ τις ἐν αὐτῇ ὥσπερ παρών τις πρὸς παρόντα.

10 [3] διαιρεῖται δὲ εἰς συχνάς τε καὶ παμπόλλους προσηγορίας. οὐ γὰρ ἐπειδὴ ἐπιστολὴ προσαγορεύεται ἑνικῷ ὀνόματι, ἤδη καὶ πασῶν τῶν κατὰ τὸν βίον φερομένων ἐπιστολῶν εἷς τίς ἐστι χαρακτὴρ καὶ μία προσηγορία, ἀλλὰ διάφοροι, καθὼς ἔφην.

[4] Εἰσὶ δὲ πᾶσαι αἱ προσηγορίαι αἷς ὁ ἐπιστολιμαῖος ὑποβάλλεται
15 χαρακτήρ, αἵδε· α΄ παραινετική, β΄ μεμπτική, γ΄ παρακλητική, δ΄ συστατική, ε΄ εἰρωνική, ϛ΄ εὐχαριστική, ζ΄ φιλική, η΄ εὐκτική, θ΄ ἀπειλητική, ι΄ ἀπαρνητική, ια΄ παραγγελματική, ιβ΄ μεταμελητική, ιγ΄ ὀνειδιστική, ιδ΄ συμπαθητική, ιε΄ θεραπευτική, ιϛ΄ συγχαρητική, ιζ΄ παραλογιστική, ιη΄ ἀντεγκληματική, ιθ΄ ἀντεπισταλτική, κ΄ παροξυν-
20 τική, κα΄ παραμυθητική, κβ΄ ὑβριστική, κγ΄ ἀπαγγελτική, κδ΄ σχετλιαστική, κε΄ πρεσβευτική, κϛ΄ ἐπαινετική, κζ΄ διδασκαλική, κη΄ ἐλεγκτική, κθ΄ διαβλητική, λ΄ ἐπιτιμητική, λα΄ ἐρωτηματική, λβ΄ παραθαρρυντική, λγ΄ ἀναθετική, λδ΄ ἀποφαντική, λε΄ σκωπτική, λϛ΄ μετριαστική, λζ΄ αἰνιγματική, λη΄ ὑπομνηστική, λθ΄ λυπητική, μ΄ ἐρω-
25 τική, μα΄ μικτή.

---

*Text: *Libanii Opera*. Ed. by R. Foerster (Leipzig: Teubner, 1927). Vol. 9.

Pseudo Libanius

Epistolary Styles   *(fourth–sixth centuries A. D.)*

[1] The epistolary style is varied and divided into many parts. It is therefore fitting that someone who wishes to write letters not do so artlessly or indifferently, but with the greatest precision and skill. One could write in the best possible style if he knew what an epistle was, what, generally speaking, custom allowed one to say in it, and into what types it was divided.

[2] A letter, then, is a kind of written conversation with someone from whom one is separated, and it fulfills a definite need. One will speak in it as though one were in the company of the absent person.

[3] It is divided into a great number of types, for the fact that a letter is designated by that single name does not mean that all letters commonly so called are of one style and one type. As I have said, they differ from one another.

[4] The following are all the types into which the epistolary style is divided: (1) paraenetic, (2) blaming, (3) requesting, (4) commending, (5) ironic, (6) thankful, (7) friendly, (8) praying, (9) threatening, (10) denying, (11) commanding, (12) repenting, (13) reproaching, (14) sympathetic, (15) conciliatory, (16) congratulatory, (17) contemptuous, (18) counter-accusing, (19) replying, (20) provoking, (21) consoling, (22) insulting, (23) reporting, (24) angry, (25) diplomatic, (26) praising, (27) didactic, (28) reproving, (29) maligning, (30) censorious, (31) inquiring, (32) encouraging, (33) consulting, (34) declaratory, (35) mocking, (36) submissive, (37) enigmatic, (38) suggestive, (39) grieving, (40) erotic, (41) mixed.

[5] Παραινετικὴ μὲν οὖν ἐστι δι' ἧς παραινοῦμέν τινι προτρέποντες αὐτὸν ἐπί τι ὁρμῆσαι ἢ καὶ ἀφέξεσθαί τινος. ἡ παραίνεσις δὲ εἰς δύο διαιρεῖται, εἴς τε προτροπὴν καὶ ἀποτροπήν. ταύτην δέ τινες καὶ συμβουλευτικὴν εἶπον οὐκ εὖ, παραίνεσις γὰρ συμβουλῆς διαφέρει. παραίνεσις μὲν γάρ ἐστι λόγος παραινετικὸς ἀντίρρησιν οὐκ ἐπιδεχόμενος, οἷον ὡς εἴ τις εἴποι, ὅτι δεῖ τὸ θεῖον τιμᾶν· οὐδεὶς γὰρ ἐναντιοῦται τῇ παραινέσει ταύτῃ μὴ πρότερον μανείς· συμβουλὴ δ' ἐστι λόγος συμβουλευτικὸς ἀντίρρησιν ἐπιδεχόμενος, οἷον ὡς εἴ τις εἴποι, ὅτι δεῖ πολεμεῖν, πολλὰ γάρ ἐστι τὰ ἐκ πολέμου κέρδη, ἕτερος δέ τις ἂν ἀντείποι, ὡς οὐ δεῖ πολεμεῖν, πολλὰ γάρ ἐστι τὰ ἐκ πολέμου συμβαίνοντα, οἷον ἧττα, αἰχμαλωσία, πληγαί, πολλάκις καὶ πόλεως κατασκαφή.

[6] Μεμπτικὴ δ' ἐστὶ δι' ἧς μεμφόμεθά τινα.

[7] παρακλητικὴ δι' ἧς ἀξιοῦμέν τινα διά τι πρᾶγμα.

[8] συστατικὴ δι' ἧς συνιστῶμέν τινα παρά τινι. ἡ δ' αὐτὴ καὶ παραθετικὴ καλεῖται.

[9] εἰρωνικὴ δι' ἧς ἐπαινοῦμέν τινα ἐν ὑποκρίσει περὶ τὴν ἀρχήν, ἐπὶ τέλει δὲ τὸν ἑαυτῶν σκοπὸν ἐμφαίνομεν, ὡς τὰ ῥηθέντα καθ' ὑπόκρισιν εἰρήκαμεν.

[10] εὐχαριστικὴ δι' ἧς χάριν γινώσκομέν τινι διά τι.

[11] φιλικὴ δι' ἧς φιλίαν ψιλὴν ἐμφαίνομεν μόνον.

[12] εὐκτικὴ δι' ἧς τυχεῖν τινος εὐχόμεθα.

[13] ἀπειλητικὴ δι' ἧς ἀπειλοῦμέν τινι.

[14] ἀπαρνητικὴ δι' ἧς ἀπαρνούμενοί τι φαινόμεθα.

[15] παραγγελματικὴ δι' ἧς παραγγέλλομέν τινι περί τινος. αὕτη δὲ καὶ μαρτυρικὴ καλεῖται.

[16] μεταμελητικὴ δι' ἧς δοκοῦμεν μεταγινώσκειν ἐφ' οἷς ὑπεσχόμεθά τινι ἢ καὶ ἐφ' οἷς ἐδόξαμεν ἐσφάλθαι.

[17] ὀνειδιστικὴ δι' ἧς ὀνειδίζομέν τινα ἐφ' οἷς ὑφ' ἡμῶν πέπονθε καλῶς, εἰ ἀμνημονεῖ.

[18] συμπαθητικὴ δι' ἧς δοκοῦμέν τινι συμπάσχειν ἐφ' οἷς ὑπέστη κακοῖς.

[19] θεραπευτικὴ δι' ἧς θεραπεύομέν τινα λυπηθέντα πρὸς ἡμᾶς περί τινος. ταύτην δὲ καὶ ἀπολογητικὴν τινες καλοῦσιν.

[20] συγχαρητικὴ δι' ἧς συγχαίρομέν τινι εὖ πράττοντι.

[21] παραλογιστικὴ δι' ἧς ὑπερφρονοῦμέν τινος ὡς εὐτελοῦς.

[5] The paraenetic style is that in which we exhort someone by urging him to pursue something or to avoid something. Paraenesis is divided into two parts, encouragement and dissuasion. Some also call it the advisory style, but do so incorrectly, for paraenesis differs from advice. For paraenesis is hortatory speech that does not admit of a counter-statement, for example, if someone should say that we must honor the divine. For nobody contradicts this exhortation were he not mad to begin with. But advice is advisory speech that does admit of a counter-statement, for example, if someone should say that we must wage war, for much can be gained by war. But someone else might counter that we should not wage war, for many (bad) things result from war, for example, defeat, captivity, wounds, and frequently the razing of a city.

[6] The blaming style is that in which we blame someone.

[7] The requesting style is that in which we make a request of someone in consequence of something important.

[8] The commending style is that in which we commend someone to someone. It is also called the introductory style.

[9] The ironic style is that in which we feign praise of someone at the beginning, but at the end display our real aim, inasmuch as we had made our earlier statements in pretense.

[10] The thankful style is that in which we express thanks to someone for something.

[11] The friendly style is that in which we exhibit simple friendship only.

[12] The praying style is that in which we pray that we may attain something.

[13] The threatening style is that in which we threaten someone.

[14] The denying style is that in which we appear to be denying something.

[15] The commanding style is that in which we command someone about something. It is also called the protesting style.

[16] The repenting style is that in which we seem to change our minds about what we had promised someone or about what we seem to have failed in.

[17] The reproachful style is that in which we reproach someone if he forgets how he has been benefited by us.

[18] The sympathetic style is that in which we seem to sympathize with someone in the misfortune that befell him.

[19] The conciliatory style is that in which we conciliate someone who has been caused grief by us for some reason. Some also call this the apologetic style.

[20] The congratulatory style is that in which we congratulate someone who is experiencing good fortune.

[21] The contemptuous style is that in which we look down upon someone as worthless.

[22] ἀντεγκληματικὴ δι᾽ ἧς ἐγκαλούμενοι ἀντεγκαλοῦμέν τινι τὸ ἐπιφερόμενον ἡμῖν ἔγκλημα περιτρέποντες τῷ ἐγκαλοῦντι.

[23] ἀντεπισταλτικὴ δι᾽ ἧς πρὸς τὰ γραφέντα ἡμῖν ἐπιστέλλομεν.

[24] παροξυντικὴ δι᾽ ἧς ἐρεθίζομέν τινα καὶ παροξύνομεν πρὸς τὴν κατά τινος μάχην.

[25] παραμυθητικὴ δι᾽ ἧς παραμυθούμεθά τινα ἐπὶ τοῖς συμβᾶσιν αὐτῷ λυπηροῖς.

[26] ὑβριστικὴ δι᾽ ἧς ὑβρίζομέν τινα διά τι.

[27] ἀπαγγελτικὴ δι᾽ ἧς ἀπαγγέλλομέν τι τῶν συμβάντων πραγμάτων.

[28] σχετλιαστικὴ δι᾽ ἧς σχετλιάζοντές τε καὶ ὀδυρόμενοι φαινόμεθα.

[29] πρεσβευτικὴ δι᾽ ἧς πρεσβεύομεν περί τινος.

[30] ἐπαινετικὴ δι᾽ ἧς ἐπαινοῦμέν τινα ἐπ᾽ ἀρετῇ τινι διαπρέποντα. χρὴ δὲ γινώσκειν ὡς ἔπαινος ἐγκωμίου διαφέρει. ἔπαινος μὲν γάρ ἐστι λόγος ἐπαινετικὸς μίαν πρᾶξιν ἐπαινῶν, ἐγκώμιον δὲ λόγος ἐγκωμιαστικὸς πολλὰς ἐν ἑαυτῷ πράξεις περιλαμβάνων. ἡ οὖν ἐπιστολὴ ἡ μίαν πρᾶξιν ἐπαινοῦσά τινος ἐπαινετικὴ καλεῖται, ἡ δὲ πολλὰς ἐγκωμιαστική.

[31] διδασκαλικὴ δι᾽ ἧς διδάσκομέν τινα περί τινος.

[32] ἐλεγκτικὴ δι᾽ ἧς ἐλέγχομέν τινα ἀρνούμενον πρᾶξίν τινα πραχθεῖσαν αὐτῷ ἢ λόγον λεχθέντα.

[33] διαβλητικὴ δι᾽ ἧς διαβάλλομέν τινα ἐφ᾽ οἷς ἔπραξεν.

[34] ἐπιτιμητικὴ δι᾽ ἧς ἐπιτιμῶμέν τινι ἐφ᾽ οἷς ἀσέμνως πράττει.

[35] ἐρωτηματικὴ δι᾽ ἧς ἐρωτῶμέν τινα περί τινος ἀγνοοῦντες ἐπὶ τῷ τὴν ἐπιστήμην εὐτυχῆσαι παρ᾽ αὐτοῦ τοῦ ζητουμένου.

[36] παραθαρρυντικὴ δι᾽ ἧς παραθαρρύνομέν τινα καὶ ἄφοβον καθιστῶμεν.

[37] ἀναθετικὴ δι᾽ ἧς τὴν ἑαυτῶν γνώμην ἀνατιθέμεθά τινι τῶν φίλων συμβουλῆς παρ᾽ αὐτοῦ δεόμενοι.

[38] ἀποφαντικὴ δι᾽ ἧς ἀποφαινόμεθα καὶ ἀπότομον κρίσιν ἐκφέρομεν κατά τινος.

[39] σκωπτικὴ δι᾽ ἧς σκώπτομέν τινα ἐπί τινι.

[40] μετριαστικὴ δι᾽ ἧς μετριάζομέν τι καὶ ταπεινοφρονοῦμεν.

[41] αἰνιγματικὴ δι᾽ ἧς ἄλλα μέν τινα λέγεται, ἄλλα δὲ νοεῖται.

[22] The counter-accusing style is that in which we bring a countercharge against someone by accusing him of what is brought against us, thus turning the charge around upon the accuser.

[23] The replying style is that in which we reply to what has been written to us.

[24] The provoking style is that in which we arouse someone to anger and provoke him to fight against someone.

[25] The consoling style is that in which we console someone over the troubles that befell him.

[26] The insulting style is that in which we insult someone for some reason.

[27] The reporting style is that in which we give some report of the things that have transpired.

[28] The angry style is that in which we appear to be angry and wailing.

[29] The diplomatic style is that in which we are diplomatic about something.

[30] The praising style is that in which we praise someone eminent in virtue. We should recognize that praise differs from an encomium. For praise is laudatory speech praising one thing, but an encomium is encomiastic speech embracing many things in itself. Therefore, the letter that praises one thing is called laudatory, and that which praises many features is called encomiastic.

[31] The didactic style is that in which we teach something to someone.

[32] The reproving style is that in which we reprove someone who denies that he has done something or said something.

[33] The maligning style is that in which we attack someone's character for what he has done.

[34] The censorious style is that in which we censure someone for what he has done indecently.

[35] The inquiring style is that in which we ask someone about something we do not know in order to obtain knowledge from him about what it is that we are inquiring about.

[36] The encouraging style is that in which we encourage someone and make him fearless.

[37] The consulting style is that in which we communicate our own opinion to one of our friends and request his advice on the matter.

[38] The declaratory style is that in which we render and carry out harsh judgment against someone.

[39] The mocking style is that in which we mock someone for something.

[40] The submissive style is that in which we are somewhat submissive and humble.

[41] The enigmatic style is that in which some things are said, but others are understood.

[42] ὑπομνηστικὴ δι᾿ ἧς δοκοῦμέν τινα τοῦ ζητουμένου πράγματος ἡμῖν ὑπομιμνήσκειν τὸν σκοπὸν ἡμῶν ἐν αὐτῇ χαράττοντες.

[43] λυπητικὴ δι᾿ ἧς ἐμφαίνομεν ἑαυτοὺς λυπουμένους.

[44] ἐρωτικὴ δι᾿ ἧς ἐρωτικοὺς πρὸς τὰς ἐρωμένας προσφερόμεθα
5   λόγους.

[45] μικτὴ δὲ ἣν ἐκ διαφόρων χαρακτήρων συνιστῶμεν.

[46] Αὗται μὲν οὖν εἰσιν αἱ προσηγορίαι πᾶσαι εἰς ἃς ἡ ἐπιστολὴ διαιρεῖται. δεῖ δὲ τὸν ἀκριβῶς ἐπιστέλλειν ἐθέλοντα μὴ μόνον τῇ τῆς ὑποθέσεως μεθόδῳ χρῆσθαι, ἀλλὰ καὶ φράσεως ἀρετῇ τὴν ἐπιστολὴν
10   κατακοσμεῖν καὶ ἀττικίζειν μὲν μετρίως, μὴ μέντοι πέρα τοῦ προσήκοντος κομψολογίᾳ χρῆσθαι. [47] ἡ γὰρ ὑπὲρ τὸ δέον ὑψηγορία καὶ τὸ ταύτης ὑπέρογκον καὶ τὸ ὑπεραττικίζειν ἀλλότριον τοῦ τῶν ἐπιστολῶν καθέστηκε χαρακτῆρος, ὡς πάντες οἱ παλαιοὶ μαρτυροῦσι, Φιλόστρατος δὲ ὁ Λήμνιος μάλιστά φησι· δεῖ γὰρ τὴν τῆς ἐπιστολῆς
15   φράσιν τῆς μὲν συνηθείας ἀττικωτέραν εἶναι, τοῦ δὲ ἀττικισμοῦ συν- ηθεστέραν καὶ μήτε λίαν ὑψηλὴν μήτε ταπεινὴν ἄγαν, ἀλλὰ μέσην τινά. [48] κοσμεῖν δὲ δεῖ τὴν ἐπιστολὴν σαφηνείᾳ τε μάλιστα καὶ συν- τομίᾳ μεμετρημένῃ καὶ ἀρχαϊσμῷ λέξεων. σαφήνεια γὰρ ἀγαθὴ μὲν ἡγεμὼν παντὸς λόγου, μάλιστα δὲ ἐπιστολῆς. [49] χρὴ μέντοι μήτε
20   συντομίᾳ σαφήνειαν διαφθείρειν μήτε σαφηνείας φροντίζοντα ληρεῖν ἀμέτρως, ἀλλὰ τοῦ συμμέτρου στοχάζεσθαι τοὺς ἀκριβεῖς τοξότας μι- μούμενον. ὥσπερ γὰρ οὔτε τὸ πολὺ τὸν προκείμενον τοῖς τοξόταις σκοπὸν παρέρχεσθαι οὔτε τὸ ἐντὸς τοῦ σκοποῦ τοξεύειν καὶ πολὺ τοῦ προσήκοντος ἀποδεῖν ἀνδρός ἐστιν εὐφυοῦς τε καὶ στοχαστικοῦ,
25   ἀλλὰ μόνου τοῦ συμμέτρως στοχαζομένου τοῦ σκοποῦ καὶ τοῦτον βάλλοντος, οὕτως οὔτε τὸ πέρα τοῦ προσήκοντος ληρεῖν οὔτε τὸ βραχυλογίαν ἀσπάζεσθαι δι᾿ ἀπορίαν καὶ τὸ σαφὲς ἐπικρύπτειν τῶν ἐπιστάλσεων ἀνδρός ἐστι λογίου, ἀλλὰ μόνου τοῦ μετ᾿ εὐφραδείας τῆς συμμετρίας στοχαζομένου καὶ τὸ λεγόμενον καλῶς σαφηνίζοντος.
30   [50] τὸ μὲν οὖν μέγεθος τῆς ἐπιστολῆς ὡς πρὸς τὰ πράγματα, καὶ οὐ πάντως τὸ πλῆθος καθάπερ κακίαν ἀτιμάζειν καλόν, ἀλλὰ δεῖ καί τινας ἐπιστολὰς ἀπομηκύνειν ἐν καιρῷ πρὸς τὴν ἀπαιτοῦσαν χρείαν, πληρώσει δὲ τὴν εἰς ἐπιστολὰς χάριν ἱστοριῶν τε καὶ μύθων μνήμη καὶ παλαιῶν συγγραμμάτων καὶ παροιμιῶν εὐστόχων καὶ φιλοσόφων
35   δογμάτων χρῆσις, οὐ μέντοι γε ταύτην διαλεκτικῶς προσακτέον.

[42] The suggestive style is that in which we seem to make a suggestion to someone in response to an inquiry directed to us, while (actually) stamping it with our own aim.

[43] The grieving style is that in which we present ourselves as being grieved.

[44] The erotic style is that in which we offer amorous words to lovers.

[45] The mixed style is that which we compose from many styles.

[46] These, then, are all the types into which the letter is divided. It is necessary that the person who wishes to write with precision not only use the proper mode of treating the subject matter, but that he also adorn the letter with excellence of style, and use the Attic style with moderation without, of course, falling into an unbecoming preciousness of speech. [47] For excessive loftiness of speech, verbosity, and Atticism are foreign to epistolary style, as all of the ancients testify. Philostratus of Lemnos says it best: "Epistolary style should be more Attic than everyday speech, but more ordinary than Atticism, and it should be neither excessively elevated nor mean, but somewhere between the two. [48] One should adorn the letter, above all, with clarity, and with moderate conciseness and with archaism in style. For while clarity is a good guide for all discourse, it is especially so for a letter." [49] In any case, one should not destroy clarity with conciseness nor chatter on immoderately while being attentive [to the need for] clarity, but should aim at moderation by imitating accurate archers. A man who is clever and skilled at hitting the target does not far overshoot the target and so widely miss what is at hand. Only the man who takes aim at the target in a properly measured manner hits it. In the same way, an eloquent man does not chatter on unbecomingly, nor does he cling to terseness in speech because he is at a loss (as to how to express himself) to the point that he obscures the clarity of his letters. Only the man who aims at due proportion while expressing himself eloquently articulates clearly what is being said. [50] The length of the letter must be determined by its subject matter, and in no way should fulness of treatment be regarded as a fault. It is, indeed, occasionally necessary to draw out certain letters as need demands. Mentioning works of history and fables will lend charm to letters, as will the use of venerable works, well-aimed proverbs, and philosophers' doctrines, but they are not to be used in an argumentative manner.

[51] Τοσαῦτα μὲν περὶ ἐπιστολιμαίου χαρακτῆρος εἰρηκὼς καὶ τοῖς λεχθεῖσιν ἀρκεῖσθαι κρίνας τοὺς συνετοὺς ὑπογράψομαι καὶ τὰς ἐπιστολὰς ἑκάστῃ οἰκείαν ἁρμόσας προσηγορίαν. προσήκει μέντοι τῷ γράφειν βουλομένῳ πρὸς τοῦ κατὰ τὴν ἐπίσταλσιν χαρακτῆρος μὴ
5 ληρεῖν μήτε μὴν ἐπιθέτοις ὀνόμασι χρῆσθαι, ὡς ἂν μὴ κολακεία τις καὶ δυσγένεια προσῇ τῷ γράμματι, ἀλλ' οὕτως ἀπάρχεσθαι· ὁ δεῖνα τῷ δεῖνι χαίρειν. οὕτω γὰρ ἅπαντες οἱ ἐπὶ σοφίᾳ τε καὶ λόγοις διαπρέψαντες παλαιοὶ φαίνονται πεποιηκότες καὶ δεῖ τὸν ἐκείνων ζηλωτὴν βουλόμενον γίνεσθαι κατόπιν αὐτῶν βαίνειν. εἰσὶ δὲ αἱ προ-
10 ταγεῖσαι ἐπιστολαὶ αὗται.

[52] Παραινετική. Ζηλωτὴς ἀεί, βέλτιστε, γενοῦ τῶν ἐναρέτων ἀνδρῶν. κρεῖττον γάρ ἐστι τοὺς ἀγαθοὺς ζηλοῦντα καλὸν ἀκούειν ἢ φαύλοις ἑπόμενον ἐπονείδιστον εἶναι τοῖς πᾶσιν.

[53] Μεμπτική. Οὐ καλῶς ἔδρασας τοὺς εὖ ποιήσαντας ἀδικήσας.
15 δέδωκας γὰρ ἄλλοις κακίας παράδειγμα τοὺς εὐεργέτας ὑβρίζων.

[54] Παρακλητική. Καὶ πάλαι μὲν ἠξίωσα τὴν σὴν ἱερὰν διάθεσιν καὶ νῦν δὲ ἀξιῶ τυχεῖν τοῦδε τοῦ πράγματος καὶ εὖ οἶδ' ὅτι τεύξομαι. δίκαιον γάρ ἐστι τοὺς γνησίους φίλους τυγχάνειν τῶν αἰτήσεων, ὅταν αὗται μὴ πονηραὶ πεφύκωσι, μάλιστα.

20 [55] Συστατική. Τὸν τιμιώτατον καὶ περισπούδαστον ἄνδρα τόνδε δεξάμενος ξενίσαι μὴ κατοκνήσῃς σεαυτῷ πρέποντα πράττων κἀμοὶ κεχαρισμένα.

[56] Εἰρωνική. Λίαν ἄγαμαι τὴν σὴν ἐπιείκειαν, ὅτι οὕτω ταχέως μεταβάλλῃ ἀπ' εὐνομίας εἰς τὸ ἐναντίον, ὀκνῶ γὰρ εἰπεῖν εἰς μοχθη-
25 ρίαν. ὡς δὲ ἔοικεν, οὐ τοὺς ἐχθροὺς φίλους ποιεῖν παρεσκεύασαι, ἀλλὰ τοὺς φίλους ἐχθρούς. τὸ γὰρ δρᾶμα δέδειχεν ὡς καὶ φίλων ἀνάξιον καὶ τῆς σῆς παροινίας ἐπάξιον.

[57] Εὐχαριστική. Πολλῶν μὲν καὶ ἄλλων ἀγαθῶν ἕνεκα χάριν γινώσκω τῇ σῇ καλοκἀγαθίᾳ, μάλιστα δὲ τοῦδε τοῦ πράγματος ἐφ' ᾧ
30 με τῶν ἄλλων ὑπὲρ ἁπάντων ὠφέλησας πλεῖον.

[58] Φιλική. Γνησίων εὐπορήσας γραμματηφόρων ἐσπούδασα τὴν σὴν ἀγχίνοιαν προσειπεῖν. ὅσιον γὰρ ὑπάρχει τοὺς γνησίους φίλους παρόντας μὲν τιμᾶν, ἀπόντας δὲ προσερεῖν.

[59] Εὐκτική. Εἴθε μοι τὸ θεῖον παράσχοι τὴν σὴν ἱερὰν θεάσασθαι
35 μορφήν, ἧς ἀπολαῦσαι πάλαι ἐλπίζω διηνεκῶς εὐχὰς ὑπὲρ τούτου ποιούμενος τῷ κρείττονι.

[60] Ἀπειλητική. Εὖξαι πάσῃ ψυχῇ καὶ παντὶ σθένει μὴ παρα-γένωμαι. ἐὰν γὰρ παραγένωμαι, πολλῶν πειραθήσῃ κακῶν, ὧν οὐκ ἤλπισάς ποτε δέξασθαι πεῖραν.

[51] Having said this about the epistolary style, and judging that what has been said will suffice for intelligent men, I shall also add the letters, joining the proper identifying name to each. Nevertheless, it befits someone who wishes to add an address to the letter type, not to chatter on, indeed, not (even) to use adjectives, lest any flattery and meanness be attached to the letter. It should begin as follows: "So-and-so to So-and-so, greeting." For thus all the ancients who were eminent in wisdom and eloquence appear to have done, and someone who wishes to emulate them must follow their example. These are the aforementioned letters:

[52] The paraenetic letter. Always be an emulator, dear friend, of virtuous men. For it is better to be well spoken of when imitating good men than to be reproached by all men while following evil men.

[53] The blaming letter. You did not act well when you wronged those who did good to you. For by insulting your benefactors you provided an example of evil to others.

[54] The requesting letter. As in the past I held your sacred friendship in high esteem, so now I expect to receive what I am requesting, and I know full well that I shall receive it! For it is right that genuine friends receive what they request, especially when they are not malicious.

[55] The letter of commendation. Receive this highly honored and much sought-after man, and do not hesitate to treat him hospitably, thus doing what behooves you and what pleases me.

[56] The ironic letter. I am greatly astonished at your sense of equity, that you have so quickly rushed from a well-ordered life to its opposite—for I hesitate to say to wickedness. It seems that you have contrived to make, not friends out of your enemies, but enemies out of your friends. For your action has shown itself to be unworthy of friends, but eminently worthy of your drunken behavior.

[57] The letter of thanks. For many other good gifts am I grateful to your excellent character, but especially for that matter in which you benefitted me above all others.

[58] The friendly letter. Since I have many sterling letter carriers available, I am eager to address your intelligent mind. For it is a holy thing to honor genuine friends when they are present, and to speak to them when they are absent.

[59] The prayerful letter. May God grant that I behold your holy form, in which I have long hoped to delight. For this I constantly offer my prayers to almighty God.

[60] The threatening letter. Pray with all your soul and strength that I not come. For if I did come, you would experience many evils you had hoped never to experience.

[61] Ἀπαρνητική. Οὐδὲν εἴργασμαι, βέλτιστε ἀνδρῶν, ὧν ἀκηκοὼς
ἐγκαλεῖς μοι δεινῶν. ὅθεν μηδὲν φαῦλον φρόνει περὶ ἐμοῦ. οὐ γὰρ
θέμις διαβολῇ πιστεύειν καὶ φήμῃ ματαίᾳ μηδὲν ὑγιὲς λεγούσῃ. διαβολὴ γὰρ μήτηρ ἐστὶ πολέμου.

[62] Παραγγελματική. Πολλάκις ἠδίκησας τὸν ἡμέτερον γεωργὸν
ὡς μὴ γινώσκων εἰς ἡμᾶς ἀνατρέχουσαν τὴν ὕβριν. ἀλλὰ παῦσαι τοῦ
λοιποῦ, μή σε καὶ τῆς προτέρας ἀδικίας δίκην εἰσπραξώμεθα.

[63] Μεταμελητική. Οἶδα καὶ σφαλείς, ὡς κακῶς διεπραξάμην. διὸ
μεταγνοὺς ἐπὶ τῷ σφάλματι συγγνώμην αἰτῶ. ἧς μεταδοῦναί μοι μὴ
κατοκνήσῃς. δίκαιον γάρ ἐστι συγγινώσκειν πταίουσι τοῖς φίλοις, ὅτε
μάλιστα καὶ ἀξιοῦσι συγγνώμης τυχεῖν.

[64] Ὀνειδιστική. Πολλὰ καλὰ πέπονθας ὑφ᾽ ἡμῶν καὶ θαυμάζω
καθ᾽ ὑπερβολήν, πῶς οὐδενὸς τούτων μνείαν ποιεῖς, ἀλλὰ κακῶς ἡμᾶς
λέγεις, ὅπερ ἐστὶν ἀχαρίστου γνώμης. οἱ γὰρ ἀχάριστοι τῶν καλῶν
ἀμνημονοῦσι καὶ τοὺς εὐεργέτας ὡς ἐχθροὺς κακῶς ἐπὶ τούτοις δια-
τίθενται.

[65] Συμπαθητική. Σφόδρα κατὰ ψυχὴν ἠχθέσθην ἀκηκοὼς περί
τινων συμβάντων σοι δεινῶν καὶ τὸ θεῖον ἱκέτευσα τούτων ἐλεύθερόν
σε καταστῆσαι. φίλων γάρ ἐστιν εὔχεσθαι τοὺς φίλους ἀεὶ κακῶν
ἐλευθέρους ὁρᾶν.

[66] Θεραπευτική. Ἐγὼ μὲν ἐφ᾽ οἷς εἶπον λόγοις μετῆλθον ἔργῳ, τὸ
γὰρ σύνολον οὐκ ἐνόμιζόν σέ ποτε λυπηθήσεσθαι· εἰ δ᾽ ἐπὶ τοῖς
λεχθεῖσιν ἢ πραχθεῖσιν ἠχθέσθης, ἴσθι, κράτιστε ἀνδρῶν, ὡς οὐκέτι
τῶν ῥηθέντων λόγον ὅλως ποτὲ ποιήσομαι. σκοπὸς γάρ μοι θεραπεύ-
ειν ἀεὶ τοὺς φίλους ἐστὶν ἤπερ λυπεῖν.

[67] Συγχαρητική. Συγχαίρω σοι λίαν ἐφ᾽ οἷς ἀγωνισάμενος
εὐδοκίμησας εἰς τοσοῦτον ὡς καὶ γραφῇ τιμηθῆναι. συγχαίρειν γὰρ
χρὴ τοῖς φίλοις εὖ πράτουσιν ὡς καὶ συναλγεῖν λυπουμένοις.

[68] Παραλογιστική. Εἰ καὶ μέγας τις ἦσθα καὶ τῶν ἐπὶ δυνάμει
βοωμένων εἷς, ἐν οὐδενί σε μέτρῳ τὸ παράπαν ἂν περιεπτυξάμην.
πολὺ δέ γε μᾶλλόν σε νῦν οὐ προσποιοῦμαι διὰ τὴν ἀσθένειάν σου.
οὐδὲν γάρ με λυπεῖς οὐ δι᾽ ἀρετὴν τοῦ μὴ θέλειν ἀδικεῖν, ἀλλὰ τῷ
δυνάμεως ἀπορεῖν.

[69] Ἀντεγκληματική. Τί ἐγκαλεῖς ἡμῖν ὡς αἰτίοις σοι γενομένοις
συμφορᾶς καὶ οὐκ ἐγκαλεῖς σεαυτῷ τῷ κακώσαντι τὰ καθ᾽ ἡμᾶς; σὺ
γὰρ ἡμῖν αἴτιος γέγονας ἀπείρων κακῶν ὁ καὶ πολλοὺς ἄλλους
λυπήσας καὶ οὐχ ἡμεῖς σοὶ οἱ μηδένα τὸ παράπαν ἠδικηκότες ποτέ.

[61] The letter of denial. I have done none of those terrible things, most noble sir, which you listen to and accuse me of. So, do not think badly of me. For it is not right to believe a false accusation and an idle rumor that contains nothing sound. For false accusation is the mother of war.

[62] The commanding letter. You have frequently wronged your farm laborer as though you did not know that the insult (was sure to) get back to us. Stop it right away, lest we bring suit against you also for your earlier injustice.

[63] The repentant letter. I know, since I failed, that I did the job badly. Having then repented, I ask your forgiveness for my failure. Do not hesitate to grant it to me, for it is right to forgive friends when they make mistakes, and especially when they ask for forgiveness.

[64] The letter of reproach. You have received many favors from us, and I am exceedingly amazed that you remember none of them but speak badly of us. That is characteristic of a person with an ungrateful disposition. For the ungrateful forget noble men, and in addition ill-treat their benefactors as though they were enemies.

[65] The sympathetic letter. I was grieved in soul when I heard of the terrible things that had befallen you, and I besought God to free you from them. For it behooves friends to pray that they may see their friends forever free of evils.

[66] The conciliatory letter. In addition to making the statements that I did, I went on (to put them) into action, for I most certainly did not think that they would ever cause you sorrow. But if you were upset by what was said or done, be assured, most excellent sir, that I shall most certainly no longer mention what was said. For it is my aim always to heal my friends rather than to cause them sorrow.

[67] The congratulatory letter. I offer my heartiest congratulations to you on so distinguishing yourself in the contest that you were honored with a painting. For friends must congratulate their friends when they experience good fortune, and must also sympathize with them when they are in sorrow.

[68] The contemptuous letter. Even if you were someone important and a person acclaimed for his authority, in no way at all would I embrace you. So much the more do I now, because of your impotence, not claim you. For you cause me no grief at all, not because of (any) excellence in not wishing to do (me) any wrong, but because you have no power (to do so).

[69] The letter of counter-accusation. Why do you accuse us of being the causes of your misfortune, and do not blame yourself, you who have caused us evil? For it is you who have caused us endless evils and have caused sorrow to many other people as well, not we, who have never caused you any harm at all.

[70] Ἀντεπισταλτική. Δεξάμενος τὰ γράμματα τῆς σῆς γνησιότητος καὶ γνοὺς δι' αὐτῶν ὡς ἐν εὐπραγίᾳ διάγεις, λίαν ἥσθην. δι' εὐχῆς γὰρ ἔχω τοὺς φίλους εὖ πράττειν ἀεί.

[71] Παροξυντική. Εἰ πόρρω τυγχάνων ἐγὼ τοῦ κακοδαίμονος Διοκλέους λίαν ἄχθομαι, καθὸ κακῶς σε πανταχοῦ γῆς διατίθεται, πολύ γε μᾶλλον σὺ τῆς εἰς σὲ λοιδορίας χάριν ὤφελες ἀμύνασθαι. καλὸν γάρ ἐστι τοὺς πονηροὺς μείζοσιν ὧν ἀδικοῦσι περιβάλλειν κακοῖς καὶ τὰς πολλὰς ἐπιστομίζειν φλυαρίας.

[72] Παραμυθητική . . .

[73] Ὑβριστική. Εἰ καλὸς ἦσθα, πολλοὺς ἂν εἶχες φίλους γνησίους· νῦν δ' ἐπειδὴ φαῦλος ἔφυς, εἰκότως οὐδένα κέκτησαι φίλον. ἕκαστος γὰρ τῶν ἐμφρόνων ἀνδρῶν σπουδὴν ποιεῖται τὸν ἄτοπον φεύγειν ἀεί.

[74] Ἀπαγγελτική. Πολλὰ δεινὰ τῇ νῦν ὑφ' ἡμῶν οἰκουμένῃ συμβέβηκε πόλει. πολέμου γὰρ αὐτὴν ἐμφυλίου κατειληφότος τὸ πλεῖστον αὐτῆς ἐξηφανίσθη ὡς μηδὲν διαφέρειν τῆς Σκυθῶν ἐρημίας.

[75] Σχετλιαστική. Ὦ πόσων ἡμῖν κακῶν αἴτιος γέγονεν ἡ συντυχία τοῦ κακοδαίμονος Ἑρμογένους, ὦ πόσαις συμφοραῖς καὶ δεινοῖς ἡμᾶς περιέβαλε. κρεῖττον γὰρ ἡμῖν τῷ Πλούτωνι ξυντυχεῖν ἢ τῷ τοῖς θεοῖς ἐχθρῷ.

[76] Πρεσβευτική. Ἀεὶ τῶν δωρεῶν τῆς ὑμετέρας κηδεμονίας ἀπελαύομεν. ὅθεν καὶ νῦν, ἀγαθοί, διὰ τῶνδε τῶν πρεσβειῶν ἀξιοῦμεν τοῦδε τοῦ πράγματος τυχεῖν, ὃ συνήθως ἀξιοῦσιν ἐχαρίσασθε. ἐν τούτῳ οὖν τὸ μεγαλόψυχον τῆς ὑμετέρας ἀρετῆς ἐπιδεῖξαι δυσωπήθητε.

[77] Ἐπαινετική. Ἀγχίνουν ὄντα σε καθ' ὑπερβολὴν καὶ σφόδρα συνετὸν ἐπαινῶ καὶ τιμῶ. πρέπει γὰρ τοὺς θείους ἄνδρας μὴ μόνον ἐπαινεῖν, ἀλλὰ καὶ τιμᾶν.

[78] Διδασκαλική. Μὴ νόμιζε τῶν συμβάντων σοι δεινῶν αἴτιον τὸ θεῖον γεγενῆσθαι. πανταχοῦ γὰρ τὸ θεῖον ἐλεύθερον κακῶν ὑπάρχει. τὸ γὰρ τοῖς ἄλλοις φεύγειν τὰ κακὰ παρακελευόμενον οὐκ ἂν αἴτιόν ποτέ τινι κακίας γένοιτο.

[79] Ἐλεγκτική. Οὐ λέληθας τόδε τὸ πρᾶγμα διαπραξάμενος. πολλοὺς γὰρ ἔχεις ἐλέγχους κἂν ἀρνῇ, καὶ μάλιστα τοὺς συνίστοράς σοι γεγονότας καὶ τῆς αὐτῆς σοι κεκοινωνηκότας πράξεως. ὅθεν μηδὲ τὴν τιμωρίαν ἔλπιζε διαφεύξεσθαι.

[80] Διαβλητική. Πολλῶν μοι κακῶν αἴτιος γέγονεν ὁ δεῖνα φαῦλος ἄγαν ὢν τὸν τρόπον. ὑποδὺς γάρ με καθάπερ φίλος καὶ πολλὰ καλὰ ὑπ' ἐμοῦ πεπονθὼς καὶ μὴ δυνηθεὶς τοῖς ἴσοις ἀμείψασθαι διὰ τὸ καλῶν ἀπορεῖν μεγίστοις περιέβαλε κακοῖς. φυλάττου γοῦν τοῦτον, μὴ καὶ σὺ τῶν ὁμοίων ὑπ' αὐτοῦ πειραθῇς δεινῶν.

[70] The letter of reply. When I received your letter expressing your genuine friendship, and learned from it that you are doing well, I was very pleased. For I pray that my friends may always prosper.

[71] The provoking letter. Although I happen to be far away from that miserable Diocles, I am extremely irritated because he bad-mouths you far and wide. You should much rather have defended yourself because he railed at you. For it is good to bring down greater evils upon bad men than those with which they wrong you, and (so) stop their slanders.

[72] The letter of consolation . . .

[73] The insulting letter. If you had been a noble person you would have had many genuine friends, but since you are now (so) bad, in all likelihood you have no friend at all. For every sensible person always hastens to flee from someone foul.

[74] The reporting letter. Many terrible things have befallen the city in which we are now living. Since it has been wracked by civil war, the greatest part of it has utterly disappeared, so that there is no difference between it and the Scythian desert.

[75] The angry letter. Oh, how many evils has our association with that miserable Hermogenes caused us! Oh, how many misfortunes and terrible things has he brought down upon us! It were better for us to have fallen in with Pluto than with (that) enemy of the gods!

[76] The diplomatic letter. We continue to enjoy the gifts your solicitude bestows on us. Hence, now too, gentlemen, through these appeals do we make the following request which you have customarily granted to those who make it. Be constrained, then, to show in this matter how magnificently excellent you are.

[77] The letter of praise. I praise and honor you for your astuteness and surpassing intelligence. For it is fitting, not only to praise extraordinary men, but also to honor them.

[78] The didactic letter. Do not think that God caused the terrible things that have befallen you. For God is completely free of evil. For he who orders others to flee evil would never cause evil to someone.

[79] The letter of reproof. You did not go unseen when you perpetrated this deed. For there are many who can prove your guilt, even if you should deny it, especially those who were privy to your crime and participated with you in the deed itself. Do not, therefore, expect to flee your punishment.

[80] The maligning letter. So-and-so, who has a very bad character, has caused me much harm. For, after having acted as though he were my friend, and having received many favors from me when he was not able to repay me measure for measure because he possessed no noble qualities, he brought the greatest evils down upon me. Be on your guard, therefore, against this man, lest you, too, experience terrible trials at his hands.

[81] Ἐπιτιμητική. Αἰδέσθητι λοιπὸν ἐφ᾽ οἷς ἁμαρτάνεις καὶ παῦσαι τοῦ πλημμελεῖν καὶ μὴ μελέτην ἁμαρτημάτων τὸν σὸν βίον ποιοῦ. σοῦ γὰρ ἕνεκεν ἡμεῖς αἰσχυνόμεθα.

[82] Ἐρωτηματική. Πολλὴν ζήτησιν εἰσενεγκάμενος περὶ τόδε τὸ κεφάλαιον καὶ μὴ κατειληφὼς αὐτοῦ τὴν εὕρεσιν δίκαιον ἡγησάμην διὰ τοῦδε τοῦ πρὸς ὑμᾶς ἐρωτηματικοῦ ῥήματος τὴν ἐπιστήμην τοῦ ζητουμένου παρ᾽ ὑμῶν εὐτυχῆσαι. λοιπὸν ἀξιοῦντι μηδαμῶς ἀποκνήσητε παρασχέσθαι τὴν χάριν καὶ ἐτιστῆσαι τὸ ζητούμενον.

[83] Παραθαρρυντική. Ἄφοβος ἔσο τὸ παράπαν, ἔχου δὲ σεμνῶς πολιτευόμενος διὰ τὸ τὸ θεῖον ἔχειν εὐμενές. πανταχοῦ γὰρ τὸ θεῖον τῷ ὀρθῶς βιοῦντι παρίσταται.

[84] Ἀναθετική. Δέδοκταί μοι τόδε τὸ πρᾶγμα διαπράξασθαι; διὸ καὶ τὴν ἐμαυτοῦ βουλὴν ἀνατίθεμαί σοι. ὅθεν το συμφέρον σκοπήσας ἐπίστειλον τὸ πρακτέον. ποθῶ γὰρ ἀεὶ παρὰ τῶν ἐμφρόνων δέχεσθαι γνώμας. αἱ γὰρ ἄρισται τῶν φίλων συμβουλίαι καλλίστας ἔχουσι τὰς εὐεργεσίας.

[85] Ἀποφαντική. Τὸν ἐμὸν οἰκέτην ἐβουλευσάμην τιμωρήσασθαι δι᾽ ἣν μοι κατεσκεύασεν ἐπιβουλήν. ὅθεν μή μοι παρακλήσεις προσάγειν περὶ αὐτοῦ πειρῶ. ἀδύνατον γάρ ἐστι μὴ τὴν ἐμαυτοῦ βουλὴν εἰς πέρας ἄξειν καὶ τοῦτον πάντη τε καὶ πάντως κολάσαι.

[86] Σκωπτική. Κίλικα μέν σε πρὸς ἁπάντων ἀκούω τυγχάνειν τῷ γένει, Ἰνδὸν δὲ σκοπῶν ἐφευρίσκω, καθάπερ αὐτὸς ὁ μελάντατος τοῦ σώματος κέκραγε χρώς.

[87] Μετριαστική . . .

[88] Αἰνιγματική . . .

[89] Ὑπομνηστική. Παραγενόμενος ἐν τῷδε τῷ τόπῳ καὶ ἀνερευνήσας τὸν τιμιώτατον ἄνδρα τὸν δεῖνα λέξον ἐξ ἐμοῦ τῷδε τάδε.

[90] Λυπητική. Σφόδρα καθ᾽ ὑπερβολὴν λελύπηκας τόδε τὸ πρᾶγμα διαπραξάμενος. ὅθεν ἰσχυρῶς ἄχθομαι πρὸς σὲ καὶ δυσίατόν τινα λυποῦμαι λύπην. αἱ γὰρ ἐκ φίλων εἰς φίλους γινόμεναι λῦπαι δυσθεράπευτοι λίαν τυγχάνουσι καὶ μείζους τῶν ἐχθρῶν ἔχουσι τὰς ἐπηρείας.

[91] Ἐρωτική. Ἐρῶ, ἐρῶ, νὴ τοὺς θεούς, τῆς σῆς εὐπρεποῦς τε καὶ ἐρωτικῆς μορφῆς καὶ ἐρῶν οὐκ αἰσχύνομαι. τὸ γὰρ εὐπρεποῦς ἐρᾶν οὐκ αἰσχρόν. εἰ δέ γε καὶ ψέξειέ τις ὅλως ὡς ἐρῶντα, πάλιν ὡς καλῆς ἐφιέμενον ἐπαινέσειεν.

[92] Μικτή. Οἶδα μὲν ὡς εὐσεβῶς ζῇς καὶ σεμνῶς πολιτεύῃ καὶ τῇ ἀνεπιλήπτου τε καὶ ἁγνῆς πολιτείας ἀρετῇ τὸ περιβόητον αὐτὸ τῆς φιλοσοφίας κοσμεῖς ὄνομα· καθ᾽ ἓν δὲ τοῦτο μόνον σφάλλῃ, καθὸ τοὺς φίλους κακῶς λέγεις, ὅπερ ἀποθέσθαι σε χρή. διαβολὴ γὰρ φιλοσόφοις οὐχ ἁρμόζει.

[81] The letter of censure. Well then, be ashamed for what you have done wrong, stop sinning, and do not live your life as an exercise in error. For, on account of you, we are disgraced.

[82] The letter of inquiry. Having investigated the following (rhetorical) topic extensively without grasping its *inventio*, I deemed it proper to address this inquiry to you and avail myself of your technical knowledge of the subject. So, please do not hesitate to grant (me) this favor I am asking, and give attention to my inquiry.

[83] The letter of encouragement. Be completely fearless, and hold your ground while living honorably, because God is well disposed toward you. For God everywhere helps the person who lives an upright life.

[84] The letter of consultation. I have decided on the following course of action, and therefore lay it before you. So consider its advantage, and write me what I should do. For I am always anxious to receive the opinions of intelligent men, for the excellent advice of friends contains in itself the most noble service.

[85] The letter of declaration. I have decided to punish my domestic slave because of the plot he devised against me. So, do not try to lodge appeals on his behalf with me. For it is impossible not to carry out my decision to its end and to punish this man most thoroughly.

[86] The mocking letter. I hear from everybody that you are a Cilician by birth, but when I look at you I discover an Indian, as though the blackest of skin itself self cries out.

[87] The submissive letter . . .

[88] The enigmatic letter . . .

[89] The suggestive letter. When you have arrived there and searched out that most honored gentleman, say the following to him in my name.

[90] The letter of grief. You caused me extremely much grief when you did this thing. For that reason I am very much vexed with you, and bear a grief that is difficult to assuage. For the grief men cause their friends is exceedingly difficult to heal, and holds in greater insults than those they receive from their enemies.

[91] The erotic letter. I love, by the gods, I love your beautiful and loving form, and am not ashamed for loving. For the love of beauty is not shameful. Indeed, would someone actually blame me for loving, let him rather praise me for longing for beauty.

[92] The mixed letter. I know that you live a life of piety, that you conduct yourself as a citizen in a manner worthy of respect, indeed, that you adorn the illustrious name of philosophy itself, with the excellence of an unassailable and pure citizenship. But in this one thing alone do you err, that you slander your friends. You must avoid that, for it is not fitting that philosophers engage in slander.

Indexes

Greek

Latin